Reconstruction and Black Suffrage

LANDMARK LAW CASES

&

AMERICAN SOCIETY

Peter Charles Hoffer
N. E. H. Hull
Series Editors

Titles in the series:
The Bakke *Case,* Howard Ball
The Vietnam War on Trial, Michal R. Belknap
Reconstruction and Black Suffrage, Robert M. Goldman
Flag Burning and Free Speech, Robert Justin Goldstein
The Salem Witchcraft Trials, Peter Charles Hoffer
Roe v. Wade, N. E. H. Hull and Peter Charles Hoffer
The Reconstruction Justice of Salmon P. Chase,
Harold M. Hyman
The Struggle for Student Rights, John W. Johnson
Igniting King Philip's War, Yasuhide Kawashima
Lochner v. New York, Paul Kens
Religious Freedom and Indian Rights, Carolyn N. Long
Marbury v. Madison, William E. Nelson
The Pullman Case, David Ray Papke
When the Nazis Came to Skokie, Philippa Strum
Affirmative Action on Trial, Melvin I. Urofsky
Lethal Judgments, Melvin I. Urofsky
Clergy Malpractice in America, Mark A. Weitz
Race and Redistricting, Tinsley E. Yarbrough

ROBERT M. GOLDMAN

Reconstruction and Black Suffrage

Losing the Vote in *Reese* and *Cruikshank*

UNIVERSITY PRESS OF KANSAS

Published by the University Press of Kansas (Lawrence, Kansas 66049), which was organized by the Kansas Board of Regents and is operated and funded by Emporia State University, Fort Hays State University, Kansas State University, Pittsburg State University, the University of Kansas, and Wichita State University

Library of Congress Cataloging-in-Publication Data

Goldman, Robert Michael.
   Reconstruction and black suffrage : losing the vote in Reese and Cruikshank / Robert M. Goldman.
      p. cm. — (Landmark law cases & American society)
   Includes bibliographical references and index.
   ISBN 0-7006-1068-5 (cloth : alk. paper) — ISBN 0-7006-1069-3 (pbk. : alk. paper)
      1. Afro-Americans—Suffrage—Cases. 2. Voter registration—United States—History. I. Title. II. Series.

   KF4893.G65 2001
   342.73'072'0264—dc21   00-043942

British Library Cataloguing in Publication Data is available.

Printed in the United States of America
10 9 8 7 6 5 4 3 2

FOR SANDIE

CONTENTS

The founding fathers of our nation believed that the ultimate guarantor of the people's liberty in a republican system of government was participation. The bedrock of this participation was voting. Voting not only reassured the people that they had a say in government, it protected ordinary people's rights. Only through a broad franchise could the revolutionary ideal of the sovereignty of the people be safe.

Although the federal Constitution of 1787 left regulation of voting in the hands of the state governments, the latter had already moved far beyond the highly restricted franchise in Great Britain. There, only a handful of propertied subjects of the crown could vote for members of the House of Commons. The judiciary and the executive were not elective offices. In the new states, more than one-half of free white males could vote, and the executive and judicial offices were elective. Over the course of the first decades of the nineteenth century, state constitutional conventions further reformed election laws, resulting in the enfranchisement of just about all free white men.

But a majority of Americans still could not vote in the first half of the nineteenth century. Women, slaves, Native Americans, immigrants, and some members of religious minorities were excluded from this most fundamental of all democratic privileges. Thus one can argue that one of the great themes of American politics and law is the gradual extension of the franchise to those who had been denied it.

Surely the last of the so-called Reconstruction Amendments to the Constitution ensuring the rights of the newly freed slaves, the Fifteenth Amendment, would seem to fit into this story of evolving equality and democracy. Under the amendment, no state could deny to any man the right to vote because of his race, color, or previous condition of servitude. The Republican Party, victorious in the Civil War and afterward the defender of the freedmen's rights, ensured that the amendment was ratified in the states of the former Confederacy. The Republicans assumed that the new law, joined by a number of congressional acts that criminalized violence at the polls, along with the Fourteenth Amendment's requirement that states provide equal protection and due process of the law for all citizens of the United States, would ensure that state governments protected the former slaves at the polling booth.

For a time, the freedmen of the South exercised these privileges freely and effectively, and former slaves sat alongside former masters in state legislatures and in Congress. But as Robert Goldman here sensitively, movingly, and succinctly demonstrates, the federal courts backed away from this commitment in the latter portion of the 1870s. From the moment the war ended, a handful of white southerners banded together to use violence against the freedmen. This included mobbing African Americans when they attempted to vote and passing laws that discriminated against the freedmen when they tried to register to vote.

But in the two leading voter rights cases of the 1870s, *Reese* and *Cruikshank*, the federal courts did not read the law to grant the right to vote or to impose on state governments the affirmative duty of protecting voters at the polls. Faced with overwhelming evidence that local officials turned their backs upon the black victims of this campaign of terror, federal courts waffled and then retreated, leaving the freedmen to the mercy of local mobs and hooded terrorists. Goldman gives due weight to the logic of the justices, but he also uncovers the extralegal motives for the Court's move.

The grounds the United States Supreme Court gave for this retreat may seem familiar to students of the Rehnquist Court in the 1990s. In the 1870s, the Supreme Court deferred to the authority of the states to regulate the polling places. Similarly, under a "strong" version of federalism verging on the long-discarded idea of "states' rights," the majority of the Rehnquist Court, led by the chief justice, has overturned federal statutes protecting the exercise of Native American religion against state drug laws and federal statutes protecting state workers from age discrimination.

Goldman's book is thus doubly relevant for modern readers. It reminds us what ensues when courts refuse to enforce laws guaranteeing minorities' rights, and it warns us that what happened at the end of Reconstruction can happen again. In his prize-winning study of the 1870s, historian Eric Foner called Reconstruction an "unfinished revolution." Robert Goldman proves that judgment still applies.

ACKNOWLEDGMENTS

Years ago I was advised that if I was truly serious about "doing history" I should be ready to accept a life of solitude and monastic isolation. I wonder about that. Historians have as their constant companions those about whom we write, past and present historians whose scholarly contributions we use (and, we hope, don't abuse), as well as family, friends, colleagues, and the students who share our everyday lives. It can be quite a crowd. It is therefore very gratifying to have the opportunity to thank those who have made "doing" this present work the least solitary of experiences. I have no doubt that they have made this volume a better one, while at the same time I take sole responsibility for its shortcomings. Although they are acknowledged in the bibliography, I must first express my debt to those scholars whose work has significantly informed this volume. Professors Lou Falkner Williams, Xi Wang, Joel Sipress, M. Les Benedict, Robert J. Kaczorowski, Donald G. Nieman, George Rable, Charles Fairman, and J. Morgan Kousser have all made important contributions to the field of constitutional history generally and to this book in particular. I also add the usual caveat that all differences of interpretation or errors are my own. Likewise I am grateful to the University Press of Kansas's outside readers of both my proposal and my manuscript. All were insightful and helpful, and I hope I have justified their support and their efforts to make this book better. Here too, however, I take responsibility for differences or errors in interpretation or fact. I appreciate the support of the editors of this series, Peter Hoffer and N. E. H. Hull, as well as the editor-in-chief of the University Press of Kansas, Michael Briggs, and his staff. Michael, as my father would say, is a true *mensch*.

Les Benedict read several early chapters and, as usual, gave great comments between gnashing his teeth at our differing writing styles. Other colleagues and friends likewise helped in small ways and large, and deserve mention and my thanks. They include Chris Waldrep, Judith Shafer, Ramsey Kleff, Weldon Hill,

Allen and Phyllis Entin, Karen Benedict, Harold Hyman, Mary Farmer, Barbara Terzian, my family in Chicago, and my "newer" family in Connecticut. I am also grateful to my summer softball teammates, who never let me use the writing of this book as an excuse for those easy pop flies or grounders I missed.

But most of all I want to thank my wife, best friend, ace reader, and support group of one, Dr. Sandra Guerard. This book is for you, Sandie.

Introduction

In the latter months of 1998 a rumor spread rapidly across the Internet: in the year 2007 African Americans throughout the country would lose their right to vote. The rumor apparently reached such proportions that the United States Department of Justice deemed it necessary to issue a formal denial from its own computer web page. The department's "Voting Rights Act Clarification" acknowledged that in the year 2007 the latest extension of the 1965 Voting Rights Act would expire, but emphasized that even if the act were not extended or revised, "the voting rights of African-Americans are guaranteed by the United States Constitution and the Voting Rights Act, and those guarantees are permanent and do not expire." Other leaders and spokespersons, both black and white, contributed their own denials and, not surprisingly, their own commentaries on what was going on. For some writers, the rumor was just another in a line of so-called urban legends, and its rapid spread a testimony to the growing ubiquity of computers, including among African Americans. Some commentators chose to blame the believers, as it were, emphasizing the particular susceptibility, if not the gullibility, of black people in America to this kind of paranoid rumormongering.

Almost all these accounts and postdenial analyses avoided any consideration of the historical context of African Americans and voting rights in America. Without making the rumor any less false or absurd than it was, it is also possible to speculate that the rumor's spread may indeed have had an element of rationality and historical resonance behind it. Rumors sometimes do, even on the World Wide Web. Exactly a century ago thousands of African Americans in the South were either in the process of losing or had already lost their right to vote, even as important political leaders such as South Carolinian Wade Hampton could write in a national publication that "it would be almost impossible to disfranchise the negro, and if possible, would not be carried into effect." Alone among other groups in American history, African Americans have experienced the tragedy of being extended the right to vote, exercising that right for a time, and then losing it. In this context, fears of losing that right again might not be totally irrational. The Voting Rights Act of 1965 was one of the most important pieces of congressional legislation during the civil rights movement. It brought about the addition of many thousands of African-American women and men to voter registration lists, which in turn has changed politics in the South, as well as the nation, in significant ways. Threats to that measure, whatever the source, could not be taken lightly.

The history of voting and voting rights in America has generally been told from the back end, beginning with who voted, for whom they cast their ballots, and why they voted the way they did. Historians and political scientists in recent years have become enamored of "party systems" and "critical election theory," explaining how coalitions of various voter groups contributed to any given election results. They have seemed far less interested in *how* these groups came to vote in the first place, to be able to cast that first ballot, than in what was done following their enfranchisement. The rationale behind this perspective is the assumption that from colonial times to the present the general trend in this country has been toward an ever-expanding electorate. One by one the barriers to political participation—property, residency, age, etc.—for various segments of the population have been eliminated to the point that today, most would acknowledge that we have achieved nothing short of "universal" suffrage.

For me, growing up in Chicago in the 1950s, the conventional wisdom that "everybody votes, including the tombstones" never seemed like hyperbole. But there are two significant exceptions to this: women and African Americans. Certainly, the struggle for women's suffrage was a long and difficult one, tied to and complicated by the more general "century of struggle" for women's

{ *Reconstruction and Black Suffrage* }

equality. But in one sense that battle ended with the ratification of the Nineteenth Amendment in 1919. For while it is true that full and meaningful participation by women in our political system, in terms of leadership and officeholding, remains a goal and an ideal, it is also true that since 1919 there has been no serious or formal attempt to deny women as a group their basic right to vote. And while one could argue that at least until the past few years women have been subjected to a variety of informal roadblocks to running for and holding public office, that essential first step—the right to vote—remained unchallenged.

Among the most important of the "promises" made by the national government to the former slaves in the South after the Civil War was the one embodied in the Fifteenth Amendment to the Constitution. It stated that a person's right to vote shall not be denied or abridged "on account of race, color, or previous condition of servitude." And for a period of time blacks in the South did indeed vote and hold elective office, including in the U.S. Congress. Then something happened. The Supreme Court's 1875 rulings in *United States* v. *Reese* and *United States* v. *Cruikshank* were part of that "something." These two cases represented both ends of a continuum that characterized white southerners' response to the Fifteenth Amendment and congressional legislation intended to enforce its provisions in the years after the Civil War. The *Cruikshank* case grew out of one of the most horrific single instances of racial violence in the post–Civil War years, the murder of almost one hundred blacks in Grant Parish, Louisiana, on Easter Sunday 1873. The *Reese* case began with a Lexington, Kentucky, election official's refusal to accept the vote of a black man because the man allegedly had not paid a $1.50 tax. During the late nineteenth century, and well past the middle of the next century, African Americans continued to be victimized by murder and refusal, and everything in between, in order to deny them the franchise.

Historians of America's constitutional past have by and large accepted former Supreme Court chief justice Charles Evans Hughes's dictum to the effect that the Constitution is what the judges say it is. Not surprisingly, most of these historical works trace the lines of court rulings, highlighting changing doctrines or interpretations of this or that provision of the Constitution over time. Specific court rulings are the trees, but the focus is invariably the forest. A historian who attempts to tell in detail the story of a single case, or in this instance, a pair of cases, has a special burden of justifying his or her interest in telling the tale. This is especially true in the *Reese* and *Cruikshank* decisions, inasmuch as the doctrines enunciated by the Court in these two cases have been thought to have been thoroughly, and justly, repudiated. Perhaps just how thoroughly is made evident to me almost every day as I pass the new library building on the campus in Richmond, Virginia, where I have taught for the past twenty-seven years. It is named the L. Douglas Wilder Library and Learning Resource Center, in honor of the man among whose accomplishments was to be the first elected African-American lieutenant governor, and then the first elected African-American governor, in American history. Governor Wilder accomplished this with the aid of thousands of African-American voters who a generation ago could not vote. Yet it is also true that both state and federal governments continue to deal with issues and cases involving the elective franchise and race. Moreover, even if they are not on the scale of a Grant Parish in 1873, or the Tulsa race riots in the 1920s, or the bombings and murders in the 1960s, crimes motivated by racial hatred continue to occur. The Ku Klux Klan, however small and generally impotent, is still around.

There are, then, a number of reasons why the story of these two cases merits telling. The first has to do with the period in American history in which these cases were decided. Some years ago historian Bernard Weisberger wrote an influential essay on the "dark and bloody ground" of Reconstruction historiography. The phrase itself came from Kentucky, where the *Reese* case originated, and referred to the conflict between Rebel and Yankee supporters after the Civil War. Weisberger contended that historians have battled over the nature and meaning of the years following the Civil War with as much passion and belligerence as the armies that fought one another *during* the war. One outcome of this historiographical struggle has been that the Reconstruction era itself, and the years immediately following it, tend to be looked upon with some confusion by students and teachers alike. I suspect that for a good number of my colleagues who teach the standard two-semester college U.S. history survey course, Reconstruction is what instructors never seem to be able to get to in the fall semester, and what is hurriedly touched upon at the beginning of the spring term. It is the warm-up act between the epic struggles of the Civil War battlefields and America's Gilded Age and the birth of modern industrial society. In this regard the Reconstruction election cases serve as a magnifying glass to make clearer a period of our history that has received far more interest from historians than the general public.

These decisions also illustrate an important but not always recognized aspect of our constitutional system. Congress makes laws and the Supreme Court interprets them, although some argue that the Court goes so far as to make the law as well. What neither Congress nor the Supreme Court does is actually enforce the law or those decisions interpreting the law. That responsibility is in the hands of a myriad of individuals, agencies, and institutions on all levels of government in all parts of the country. Laws may be passed, but never enforced. They may be partially enforced, or enforced in ways unforseen by those who passed them. Sometimes what the Court decides may or may not always be how individuals or groups actually experience their rulings. In this regard the Reconstruction election cases were as much about the enforcement of the right to vote as about the right itself. Shortly after ratification of the Fifteenth Amendment, Congress passed a series of laws intended to enforce the provisions of that amendment, and by so doing involved the federal government in law enforcement to a degree previously unknown. Indeed, the institution responsible for that enforcement, the Department of Justice, had itself come into being only in 1870. Today few question the necessity of even having an entire Civil Rights Division within the Justice Department. It was not always so. These cases, therefore, must be viewed as an important chapter in the development of our institutions of national law enforcement as well.

In 1937 then–attorney general Homer Cummings, along with

his assistant Carl McFarland, published *Federal Justice*, the first, and as yet only, comprehensive history of the Justice Department. In his introduction to the volume Cummings eloquently concluded that

> [a] government of laws makes heavy demands upon those who tend its administration. . . . From the safe vantage of the years we may look back upon their triumphs and mistakes. To be sure, there are sordid chapters and many unhappy and unflattering incidents in the history of federal justice. In its field, it has followed the main currents of American life. . . . Great controversies throw into relief the development and processes of government. They point the moral and illustrate the hazards ever present in the daily work of the law and in its battles on a thousand fronts.

The story of *U.S. v. Reese* and *U.S. v. Cruikshank*, as told from this "safe vantage of the years," I hope illustrates Cummings's sentiments.

CHAPTER I

"We Are Americans, We Are Citizens"

In early February of 1866 President Andrew Johnson granted an interview at the White House to a delegation of prominent African Americans, including the former slave and abolitionist leader Frederick Douglass. The group's message to the president was brief and straightforward. The recently ratified Thirteenth Amendment, abolishing slavery in all parts of the country, was not enough. As "native born Americans," the delegation now sought assurance that their rights as American citizens would be fully and equally protected. To ensure that their rights as citizens would be guaranteed, they urged that blacks everywhere be "fully enfranchised."

What they received from President Johnson was a lengthy prepared response, by turns supportive, condescending, and hostile. The freedman had no greater friend, the president claimed, but he warned that giving the black man the ballot "without preparation" would lead to renewed hostilities across the land, this time between the races. Moreover, he had no intention of going against the will of a majority of southerners, who he claimed opposed the idea, although he was pointedly reminded by Douglass that in states like South Carolina African Americans were probably in the majority. If former slaves were going to get the right to vote, Johnson advised, they must look to their state governments.

In fact, the reason for the delegation's meeting with the president was that by early 1866 it had become increasingly obvious that southern states had no intention of allowing their recently freed population access to the ballot box. For African Americans in the South the cessation of the hostilities of the Civil War in

1865 had also been a beginning. Because of the Thirteenth Amendment their lives as chattel slaves were now over, at least by law. But having fulfilled the goal of abolishing slavery, Congress now faced the thornier question of what additional protections and rights the freedmen would require. The question became especially urgent as the former Confederate states began the process of creating new state constitutions and governments under the direction of President Johnson. Under these new governments state legislatures passed what were known as "black codes," a series of laws that seemed intended to resubjugate former slaves. While these "codes" provided some basic legal rights for the freedmen, such as the right to have legally recognized marriages, own property, and make binding contracts, the primary thrust of these measures was to ensure the economic and political subordination of blacks. In the spring of 1866 Congress responded by passing the first of a series of measures designed to protect the basic legal and civil rights of the freedmen.

The Civil Rights Act of April 1866 was an important first step. It explicitly extended citizenship to African Americans and set forth a list of basic legal rights that the states, and state officials, were required to respect. But what made this act remarkable were the provisions to enforce these rights. All local federal officials, including district attorneys, marshals, and their deputies, as well as agents of the recently created federal agency known as the Freedman's Bureau, were authorized to arrest and institute criminal proceedings against anyone violating the rights specified under the act. The government not only had expanded the idea of what constituted federally protected rights, but for the first time had committed itself to actually enforcing these rights as well.

It was also obvious that the new southern state governments created under Johnson's direction had no intention of allowing former slaves any sort of political rights. Indeed, thanks to Johnson's lenient use of pardons, those who voted for and held office in these new governments, including congressional representatives, were by and large the same white men who had done so before secession. Growing numbers of Republicans, both in and out of Congress, realized that for the newly freed slaves even the

{ *Reconstruction and Black Suffrage* }

barest minimum of rights were endangered unless blacks had the right to participate in the election of their leaders and the passage of laws governing their lives. As the congressman who would be largely responsible for drafting the Fifteenth Amendment, Massachusetts Republican George Boutwell explained: "With the right of voting, everything a man ought to have or enjoy of civil rights comes to him. Without that right he is nothing." Former abolitionist leader Wendell Phillips echoed such sentiments when he wrote that "A man with a ballot in his hand is the master of the situation. He defines all his other rights. What is not now given him, he takes." And certainly African Americans recognized the importance of voting rights: hence, their visit to the White House in 1866. For while Douglass and the others were disappointed, they were hardly discouraged. That meeting had been a turning point, showing the nation Johnson's true intentions with respect to the future of the freedpeople and elevating voting rights to a national issue that from then onward "was not allowed to rest."

There were two basic arguments standing in the way of enfranchisement. First, there were those who agreed with President Johnson in believing that African Americans were not yet ready to be granted the right to vote. Having been denied by law the opportunity for education under slavery, the vast majority of black adults were illiterate, and, so the argument went, were incapable of exercising the franchise in any meaningful way. Ignoring the large number of white males, especially in the South, who were uneducated, those who made this argument assumed that blacks would be especially susceptible to bribery and fraud. They likewise argued that there was no necessary connection between the ballot box and other rights, since groups like women and children were not deprived of meaningful legal and social participation in society because they could not vote.

Another serious concern was the uncertainty over the constitutional authority of the federal government to do anything with regard to suffrage. Aside from listing the qualifications for holding national office, the Constitution was virtually silent on the role of the federal government and the right to vote. The only relevant passage was Article I, Section 4, which gave the states responsibility for determining "The times, places and manner of holding elections for Senators and Representatives," but also stated that "Congress may at any time by law make or alter such Regulations, except as to the places of choosing Senators." Prior to the Civil War, accepted constitutional doctrine held that voting qualifications and requirements were the responsibility of the states. By 1860 these primarily involved residency requirements and definitions of who was entitled to the ballot. Beginning in the 1820s, states had expanded the number of adult males eligible to vote by removing property qualifications. But certain groups, such as women, aliens, students, the insane, paupers, and criminals, were excluded. As of 1860, African Americans could vote in only five states: Maine, Vermont, New Hampshire, Rhode Island, and Massachusetts. Blacks could vote in New York if they met additional property and residency qualifications. As of 1866, President Johnson was correct in insisting that blacks should look to their states if they wanted enfranchisement.

Yet while Republicans could not be sure that there was authority in the Constitution for the federal government to extend voting rights to a particular group, they were coming more and more to the view expressed by Boutwell and Phillips that suffrage would be crucial to the success of Reconstruction. All over the South blacks themselves held mass meetings and conventions to protest the hostile and increasingly violent treatment they were receiving under President Johnson's Reconstruction efforts. Invariably they demanded the franchise as a means of protection.

Republicans in Congress responded. They first attempted to deal with the suffrage issue in the Fourteenth Amendment. First presented to Congress at the end of April 1866, the Fourteenth Amendment was intended to provide constitutional authority for the Civil Rights Act of 1866 and place civil rights beyond the power of state majorities to repeal. The first section of the amendment repeated the citizenship provisions of the act and prohibited the states from denying citizens the "equal protection of the laws" and from abridging their "privileges and immunities." Using the same language as the Fifth Amendment, the first section of the Fourteenth Amendment also prohibited states from depriving persons of their "life, liberty or property" without "due process of law." But the second section of the amendment provided that representation in the House of Representatives would be reduced for any state that "denied to any male inhabitants of such State, being twenty-one years of age, and citizens of the United States, or in any way abridged except for participation in rebellion or other crime" the right to vote in a federal election.

Together, the first two sections revealed a carrot-and-stick approach to the enfranchisement issue. With African Americans made citizens in the amendment's first section, future southern representation in Congress stood to increase substantially, since the infamous "three-fifths" clause of Article I of the Constitution, which excluded "all other persons" for apportionment purposes, would no longer apply. The second section of the amendment was the stick, an admittedly "clumsy" attempt to bribe southern states into granting voting rights to the freedmen on pain of losing that additional representation. It didn't work. Southern states refused to ratify the amendment, arguing, among other things, that it would result in "political equality" between the races. As new state governments were created under President Johnson's direction in 1866, no attempt was made to include any sort of suffrage provisions for blacks. In December 1865 Congress created a Joint Committee on Reconstruction to investigate conditions in the South. The committee discovered a widespread campaign of terror and denial of rights against blacks, including murderous riots in places such as New Orleans and Memphis. These findings plus the reelection to Congress of former Confederate leaders convinced congressional Republicans that President Johnson's Reconstruction policies were proving a failure and that Congress needed to act quickly and forcefully.

Ironically, southern rejection of the Fourteenth Amendment proved beneficial to the movement to enfranchise African Americans. Even moderate Republicans in Congress became convinced that the ballot box was crucial to any solution to the widespread terror and opposition going on throughout the

South. With congressional Republicans in a veto-proof position following the November 1866 elections, these moderates were willing to work with the more "radical" Republicans in Congress, who had been arguing that only strong federal action could prevent the South from returning to its antebellum condition. In December 1867, Congress began a series of steps that would ultimately lead to the Fifteenth Amendment. Over the space of three months, Congress enfranchised black voters in the District of Columbia, removed racial restrictions on voting in unorganized federal territories in the West, and required "impartial suffrage" as a condition for admitting the new states of Nebraska and Colorado. From at least the constitutional standpoint these measures were noncontroversial, since they were based on explicit provisions for congressional authority over the District of Columbia and federal territories. In vetoing the District of Columbia bill President Johnson used the same argument that he later made to Frederick Douglass, that African Americans were as yet "unprepared" to accept franchise responsibilities. In overriding Johnson's veto, Republicans served notice that they would be willing to use federal authority to secure voting privileges elsewhere, especially the South.

In response to the white southerners' outright rejection of the Fourteenth Amendment, Congress in March of 1867 passed the first of a series of Reconstruction Acts "to provide for the more efficient Government of the Rebel states." These measures placed the former Confederate states under military rule, made existing state governments created under President Johnson's direction provisional, and required southerners to create new governments under military supervision. Delegates to these new state constitutional conventions were to include all qualified male citizens "of whatever race, color, or previous conditions," except those disfranchised as past rebels or convicted criminals. These new state constitutions had to include suffrage provisions based on the same inclusive definition—"of whatever race"—required of convention delegates, and the states had to ratify the Fourteenth Amendment. The Reconstruction Acts explicitly acknowledged that suffrage should not be limited by race, but like the Fourteenth Amendment, the acts still took the indirect form of a precondition that was up to the states to fulfill. The difference now, however, was that any state that failed to do so would in effect be denied *any* representation in Congress.

Under the provisions of military, or congressional, Reconstruction, new state governments were created in most of the southern states. It is estimated that as a result of the neutral race sections of the Reconstruction Acts some 735,000 African-American voters were registered to cast their first ballots. They certainly did so, for the turnout in most of the states far exceeded 50 percent of those eligible. Throughout the South black candidates were elected to local and state offices. In South Carolina Joseph Rainey became the first African American to enter the House of Representatives, while Hiram Revels of Mississippi was elected to the U.S. Senate in 1870. Across the South state governments came under the control of a combination of African Americans, northerners who had come South during and after the War and stayed (the "carpetbaggers"), and native white southerners. What united these groups was their identification with the Republican Party and their support for congressional Reconstruction policies.

Yet from the very moment these new state governments began exercising authority, opposition appeared from white southerners. On one hand they attacked the very legitimacy of these "Radical regimes," arguing that Congress had unconstitutionally forced black suffrage on a politically helpless South. Echoing President Johnson's line, these white southerners complained that having just obtained freedom, African Americans were not ready to exercise the serious responsibilities of citizenship that voting entailed. Black voters and officeholders had become the unwilling dupes of unscrupulous and "rapacious" northern carpetbaggers and their treasonous henchmen, native southern white "scalawags," all of whom were bent on lining their own pockets at the public till and ensuring the continued plunder of a defeated section and people. For these white southerners the Democratic Party became the political vehicle to "redeem" their states from the hands of these corrupt, incompetent, dictatorial, "foreign" regimes.

Democratic attacks on the very legitimacy of Republican state governments served to justify any means necessary to overthrow these governments, including violence. From its beginnings in Pulaski, Tennessee, in 1866, the Ku Klux Klan became the model for paramilitary units throughout the South. Although these groups went by a variety of names—Knights of the White Camelia, the White League, and the Council of Safety—their goals and tactics were characteristically similar: the use of violence, intimidation, and terror against black voters and their Republican supporters. While the participants of the "Invisible Empire" might rationalize their deeds through references to southern traditions of preserving "honor" and combating "lawlessness" in the absence of legitimate authority, it became increasingly clear after 1867 that a chief aim of the Klan was the utter and complete destruction of the "preposterous notion of Negro equality."

In attacking black suffrage in theory and in practice, southern Democrats could also point to the element of hypocrisy in Republican policies. Was it not true, they contended, that blacks could not vote in most northern states? Indeed, in state contests in 1867–68, attempts to enfranchise African Americans were rejected in Ohio, Minnesota, Kansas, and Michigan. Some northern commentators even suggested that Republican support for equal voting rights was responsible for a surge of Democratic victories in such key states as New York, New Jersey, and Ohio. The Republican platform in the 1868 presidential election did reflect this ambivalence. It called on southern states to accept congressionally mandated suffrage requirements, while conceding that the "question of suffrage in all the loyal States properly belong(s) to the people of those States."

The results of the 1868 presidential election provided the final push leading to a suffrage amendment. Although Republican Ulysses S. Grant was victorious over his Democratic opponent, Horatio Seymour of New York, Klan activity suppressed Republican turnout across the South, and in Georgia and Louisiana it contributed to a Democratic victory. Nationwide, Grant's margin of victory in the popular vote was about 300,000, less than the total number of the estimated one-half million African Americans who voted. It had thus become clear that the political future of the Republican Party, not only in the South but nationwide, depended on black votes. Political reality converged with Republican principles, and accordingly, at the opening session of the Fortieth Congress in January 1869, proposals were submitted and debated by Congress that a month later led to the passage of the Fifteenth Amendment. By February 1870 the amendment received the assent of three-fourths of the states necessary for ratification.

As it became part of the Constitution, the Fifteenth Amendment read:

Section 1. The right of citizens of the United States to vote shall not be denied or abridged by the United States or by any State on account of race, color, or previous condition of servitude.

Section 2. The Congress shall have power to enforce this article by appropriate legislation.

An obvious question is posed by the language of Section 1: If the amendment was intended to enfranchise black voters, why did it not directly do so? Why confer a positive new right by forbidding its denial? Was the amendment primarily a partisan attempt to ensure future Republican majorities, or was it a reflection of the Republicans' commitment to racial equality and the success of Reconstruction? The consensus answer among historians and other scholars who have examined the debates and maneuvering in Congress that led to final passage is that the Fifteenth Amendment was a compromise among various interests and views within the Republican majority in Congress. The amendment was a "moderate" measure designed to satisfy a number of interests. It reflected the goals of those Republicans committed to the principles of civil and political equality for the freedmen, as well as those whose main concern was continued Republican Party dominance. The amendment also took into account those willing to limit suffrage to the literate and those who feared that a constitutional amendment would open the door to enfranchising other groups, particularly Chinese immigrants and women. Despite unsuccessful attempts to include such features as protection for "officeholding," and the explicit disfranchisement of certain categories such as ex-Confederates, the final language of the amendment was almost identical to the original proposal introduced by Illinois congressman George S. Boutwell. Thus, whatever disputes arose over who should or should not be included, the negative phraseology was not questioned. Why was the amendment worded this way? In the context of prior constitutional language, the Fifteenth Amendment's formulation was not innovative, but consistent with other federally "granted" rights. For example, the First Amendment did not "give" citizens freedom of speech. It forbade Congress from making some law that would "abridge" that particular right. The recently ratified Fourteenth Amendment did much the same thing by forbidding states to "deprive" citizens of their rights to due process and the equal protection of the laws. Indeed, all future amendments dealing with voting used the same negative phrasing: the Nineteenth and women, the Twenty-Fourth and poll taxes, and the Twenty-Sixth and eighteen-year-olds.

The response to the ratification of the Fifteenth Amendment was generally positive. President Grant went so far as to believe that with its ratification the question of black suffrage was "out of politics," and he pronounced reconstruction "completed." Former abolitionists and African-American leaders likewise applauded the amendment, and public celebrations were held in a number of cities around the country. For Frederick Douglass the amendment was the beginning of true equality for black people and assured that "color is no longer to be a calamity; that race is to be no longer a crime; and that liberty is to be the right of all." Yet amid all the celebrations and optimism there was a more sobering and realistic response. It was understood, particularly by Republicans in Congress, that by itself the Fifteenth Amendment was as much a statement of an ideal as it was a self-fulfilling new right. Concerns about the actual effect of the amendment raised during the debates over its drafting resurfaced, especially the extent to which it might or might not limit traditional state control over voter qualifications. More ominous was the fact that even as the process of ratifying the Fifteenth Amendment proceeded, Klan violence, intimidation, and murder continued against blacks and their Republican supporters throughout the South. State governments were either unwilling or unable to combat this growing terror, and in several instances appealed directly to Washington for help. In one of his first speeches as the first elected African-American senator, Hiram Revels of Mississippi made an impassioned plea for Congress to provide additional legislation to enforce the Fifteenth Amendment. Revels cited both the necessity of "protection" of the freedmen in the South and the obligation owed by the nation to black soldiers who had fought in the Union army, which had been "thinned by death and disaster."

Starting in May 1870, Republicans in Congress considered and passed a series of measures intended to enforce Section 1 of the Fifteenth Amendment, and to a lesser extent, the citizenship protections inherent in the Fourteenth Amendment. Since both amendments had specific sections that allowed for "appropriate legislation" for enforcement, there was little or no debate on the possible constitutionality of such actions. Rather, the House and Senate maneuvers over these bills, like those over the Fifteenth Amendment itself, revolved mainly around differences over methods and means of enforcement, the extent and role of federal authorities, and the application of these measures to areas other than the South. And whether these measures were the outcome of Republican "principles" or party "politics," or a combination of both, the Enforcement Acts, or Force Acts as they also came to be called, were the most comprehensive set of federal criminal statutes yet seen in the Republic. The Enforcement Acts consisted of three measures passed between May 1870 and April 1871. There were also two smaller, supplemental acts, one passed in July 1870 dealing with naturalization of citizens, and one in June 1872 involving appropriations.

The most important of these measures was the first Enforcement Act, passed on May 31, 1870. Entitled "An Act to enforce the Right of Citizens of the United States to vote in the several States of this Union, and for other purposes," it consisted of twenty-three sections and became the basis for federal suffrage protection policies for the next quarter-century, including the prosecutions in both the *Reese* and *Cruikshank* cases. Significantly, the first section of the act, unlike the Fifteenth Amendment, affirmed a positive right to vote. It stated that all citizens qualified to vote in any state or local election "shall be entitled to vote at all such elections, without distinction of race, color, or previous condition of servitude." The following several sections of the act provided specific penalties, including fines and imprisonment, for anyone convicted of preventing or attempting to prevent any person from either exercising their voting privileges or attempting to perform any of the prerequisites to voting, such as registering. Victims of voting rights infringements could also bring civil suit against those "persons or officers" who had denied them their rights, and receive up to five hundred dollars and court costs for each offense.

Provisions of the act detailed the various "unlawful means" that might "hinder, delay, prevent, or obstruct" any citizen from voting or doing anything necessary to qualify for the act of voting. These methods included, but were not necessarily limited to, "force, bribery, threats, and intimidation" of voters or potential voters. It was also illegal to use various forms of economic coercion, such as threats of loss of employment or refusals to renew labor contracts and leased or rented property agreements, as well as "threats of violence" to individuals and their "families," to prevent anyone from exercising franchise rights. That much of the actual interference with franchise rights in the South was being perpetuated by the Ku Klux Klan or Klan-type activity was clearly recognized in section 6 of the act, which made it a felony if "two or more persons shall band or conspire together, or go in disguise upon the public highway, or upon the premises of another, with intent to violate any provision of this act" or "to injure, oppress, threaten, or intimidate any citizen with intent to prevent or hinder his free exercise and enjoyment of any right or privilege granted or secured to him by the Constitution or laws of the United States." The act allowed for state prosecutions of crimes not listed or precluded by the prior two sections. Other parts of the act detailed and made criminal a variety of fraudulent methods that could be employed to deny or hinder access to the ballot, from ballot box stuffing to the registration of fictitious or dead persons.

What gave the May 1870 Enforcement Act its uniqueness were the several sections that set up the actual machinery and procedures whereby the act would be implemented. While state and local officials were made liable for following the provisions of the act, the direct responsibility for enforcing the measure was given to the federal government, specifically the Department of Justice. Department officials, including district attorneys and their assistants, marshals and their deputies, and special "commissioners of elections," were all granted authority to arrest, imprison, set bail for, and prosecute all those suspected of violating provisions of the act. These officials were themselves subject to fines for failure to obey and execute the laws, and were placed under the authority of federal district courts and district court judges. At the same time it was also made a crime for any citizen to in any way obstruct or hinder any federal officials or try to prevent them from carrying out their responsibilities under the act. Federal district courts were given "exclusive" jurisdiction over any and all crimes and offenses arising out of the enforcement legislation, and prosecutions could be brought either by federal grand jury indictment or by "informations" filed by district attorneys in federal courts.

The remaining sections of the act strengthened and expanded federal enforcement guarantees beyond suffrage protections. The Civil Rights Act of 1866 was "re-enacted," and the civil protections contained in that measure, along with the Fourteenth Amendment, were likewise now subject to the same federal enforcement machinery and jurisdiction described above for the Fifteenth Amendment. And finally, to give real "teeth" to the measure, it was made "lawful" for the president to "employ such part of the land or naval forces of the United States, or of the militia, as shall be necessary to aid in the execution of judicial process issued under this act."

The second of the three major Enforcement Acts was passed on February 28, 1871. In large part it merely amended the May 1870 measure by filling in details of what was required of federal officials charged with enforcing that act. But it also extended the reach of federal authority in several important ways. It enlarged section 20 of the 1870 act, which dealt specifically with elections for members of Congress. In cities with populations above twenty thousand persons special election "supervisors" were to be appointed. These supervisors were given extensive authority over all aspects of the actual electoral process, from registration to the final counting of votes. These officials were not merely passive observers, but could immediately call on federal marshals and their deputies to make arrests or initiate prosecutions when violations occurred. Moreover, added to the list of possible crimes was, in effect, an entire new category of offenses involving the use of "fraudulent" activities intended to deprive citizens of their franchise rights. Although the measure was primarily a response to Democratic Party outrages in northern cities in the 1870 elections, the provisions could be applied to the South as well, especially as southern Democrats took to less visible and obvious forms of negating black voting rights than outright intimidation and violence. A supplemental measure, passed in June of 1872 as part of an appropriations bill, extended the use of supervisors in places of less than twenty thousand persons, albeit with some limitations.

The third of the major enforcement measures was passed in April 1871. It was titled the Ku Klux Force Act, and as its name suggested, it intended nothing less than the outlawing of the Klan and its nefarious activities. It reenforced previous measures by extending the president's authority to prevent large-scale interference with federal authority through his suspension of the writ of habeas corpus and his power to use military force to counter domestic upheavals. It further reaffirmed the authority of federal courts to hear cases involving violations of both civil rights, as defined in the Civil Rights Act of 1866, and political rights, as set forth in the previous enforcement legislation. But the key provision was the second section, which expanded on the first enforcement act in cataloging the numerous ways "two or more persons" might "conspire" together to violate the defined civil and political rights of citizens. All these were now federal "high crimes," punishable by fines and imprisonment.

The debates and maneuvering on the Enforcement Acts revealed not only expected strenuous Democratic opposition, but some reservations among Republicans as well. Although Republicans agreed that the measures fell under the "appropriate legislation" rubric of section 2 of the Fifteenth Amendment, there was concern that the measures went beyond the "no state" language of the amendment by criminalizing individual and private actions. That the measures became so quickly referred to as the "Force Acts" signified a subtle but important shift in how they might come to be viewed. For Democrats, especially southern Democrats, the term "force" was sure to evoke images of the war, military Reconstruction, and their worst fears of a federal government's uncontrolled determination to subjugate and humiliate a defenseless people. These sentiments were expressed at the time, and much later. William W. Davis, whose 1914 account of the passage of the Enforcement Acts remained the standard historical interpretation for many years, concluded that "the enactment of the law and its enforcement meant the desertion, for the time being, by the national government of certain principles of political procedure which make working democracy in America a practical possibility." He likened the Enforcement Acts to the "mailed fist" used by England to subjugate the Irish people.

In fact, taken as a whole, the Enforcement Acts of 1870–72 were neither a "mailed fist" nor an abandonment of traditional democratic principles. For one thing, the acts were passed in response to a very real situation. By 1870 Congress had volumes of testimony, investigative reports, and other information that confirmed the fact that throughout the South a determined and often violent effort was under way, aimed not only at overthrowing the Reconstruction governments there, but at undermining and resisting the civil and political rights of American "citizens."

Both the Fourteenth and Fifteenth Amendments authorized Congress to pass "appropriate legislation" to "enforce" the provisions of those amendments. Moreover, although penalties of fines and imprisonment accompanied convictions for violation of these laws, they were hardly draconian by nineteenth-century standards. And finally, with the exception of the use of election supervisors, the Enforcement Acts set up no new government agency or police force to implement the measures. They relied on federal officials such as district attorneys and marshals, and federal court judges, who had been functioning since 1789. Thus, however radical these measures might appear, their actual implementation remained within the framework of traditional "political procedure." That would provide the greatest uncertainties.

CHAPTER 2

Enforcing the Enforcement Acts

On paper the Enforcement Acts of 1870–72 provided a comprehensive set of laws and the machinery to protect the civil and political rights of the freedman as defined by the Fourteenth and Fifteenth Amendments. But the real test would be the federal government's successful implementation of these statutes. Even the best-written laws are meaningless if they are not properly and effectively enforced, and this was certainly the case with the Enforcement Acts. With the exception of the federal revenue statutes, these measures constituted nothing less than the first national criminal code. Concerns about these measures at the outset were less about the language and wording of the laws than about this fact. Ever since colonial times criminal wrongdoing and its punishment in America had been almost entirely the responsibility of local governments and authorities, and almost one hundred years of national government had made little difference. In the minds of most Americans, particularly southerners, criminal justice meant local justice and nothing more. What actions constituted criminal wrongdoing among citizens, the penalties for such violations, and the enforcement of sanctions were community concerns, and even state authorities were often seen as outsiders to be resented and resisted. Inasmuch as the Enforcement Acts were framed as federally enforceable criminal statutes, there was as much concern about the legislation's actual implementation as there was about its constitutionality. Indeed, many questioned whether the federal government was up to the task of enforcing these laws in light of this tradition of localism.

It was an old tradition. Each of the English North American colonies in the seventeenth century developed its own criminal code as well as its own officials to enforce the code. In most of the colonies county sheriffs, and then as towns and cities grew, local constables, served as the primary law enforcement officers. This situation did not change greatly after the Revolution. State and local courts continued to enforce criminal statutes as determined by that state or locality, and judges and local juries continued to hold the reins of their enforcement. Moreover, crime and its punishment was primarily "reactive" in the sense that at least until the 1840s neither the states nor local governments had the resources or means to seek out wrongdoers and prevent wrongdoing *before* possible crimes were committed.

The tradition of localism in criminal law enforcement had important consequences. Since formal state and local law enforcement was often so inefficient, sporadic, and even corrupt, individuals felt justified in taking the law into their own hands. This became known as vigilantism. The Regulators in South Carolina in the 1760s became the prototype for this type of local "popular" justice. The Regulator movement emerged in the back country of South Carolina in response to the absence of any formal courts or colonial governmental authority, and for a number of years the Regulators exercised the only law enforcement in that part of the colony. This unique "lawless" response to lawlessness would be repeated as America's frontier expanded westward through the following century. Nor was vigilantism confined to rural or frontier areas. One of the most famous examples of the phenomenon was the San Francisco Vigilance Committee in the 1850s. One historian has identified at least 326 vigilante movements in the United States up until 1900. Moreover, many of the Ku Klux Klan organizations that appeared after the Civil War styled themselves in the Regulator tradition of popular, and local, law enforcement.

The other source of vigilantism as a response to ineffective local law enforcement was a tradition of distrust of, if not outright hostility to, any form of what might be considered "outside" authority. Early on, outside authority meant state governments, but it gradually came to include the national government as well. The best-known example of this both before and after the Civil War was the ongoing struggle between federal government revenue collectors and distillers of illegal liquor, particularly in the mountain regions of the South. The "war" between the "revenuers" and the "moonshiners" would become the stuff of overblown legend. But the failures of the federal government to combat this problem were very often the result of local sympathy for, if not actual participation in, the manufacture and distribution of the product.

Under the provisions of the May 1870 Enforcement Act, the federal Department of Justice and federal district courts were given "cognizance over all crimes and offences committed against the provisions of this act." Similar jurisdictional responsibility was provided in the subsequent enforcement legislation as well. Significantly, the Department of Justice itself was brand-new, having been formally created by Congress in June of 1870. Any understanding of the success or failure of the protection of African-American voting rights in the South both during and after Reconstruction must therefore begin with the background and context within which the department itself came into being and functioned.

The 1870 legislation creating the Department of Justice reformed and expanded an already existing national office. Under the Judiciary Act of 1789, which created the federal judicial system, provision was made for a "meet person learned in the law" to serve as "attorney general for the United States." The function of this official was twofold. The attorney general would "conduct and prosecute" all suits before the Supreme Court to which the United States was a party and would provide "advice and opinion" on legal questions presented by either the president or the heads of other government departments. In addition, in each of the lower federal court districts created under the Judiciary Act there was also to be appointed a "government attorney," who would, with the assistance of a federal marshal, prosecute cases on behalf of the national government. Like all other members of the federal judiciary, these officials would be appointed by the president with the approval of the Senate. President George Washington appointed fellow Virginian Edmund

Randolph as the first attorney general. Among Randolph's prime qualifications for the position was the fact that he had served as Washington's personal attorney for many years, thus setting a precedent for future nominees that would continue to the present. As attorney general, Randolph had no staff to assist him, and felt free to supplement his salary of fifteen hundred dollars a year by continuing his private legal practice. Although the position was not formally recognized as part of what became the president's cabinet, Randolph was invited by Washington to regularly attend cabinet meetings, and this practice continued with attorneys general up to 1870. Randolph had no illusions about the significance of his office, describing it as "a sort of mongrel between the States and the U.S.; called an officer of some rank under the latter, and yet thrust out to get a livelihood in the former." Most of his official activities involved providing advice and rendering legal opinions when requested by other federal officials.

Over the next sixty years changes in the office of attorney general were generally due to the efforts of particularly able incumbents. Most notable among these were William Wirt and Caleb Cushing. Appointed by President James Monroe in 1817, Wirt would become the longest-serving attorney general, leaving office in 1829. Upon taking office, Wirt discovered that in the years since fellow Virginian Randolph held the attorney generalship the office had pretty much remained a "one-man operation." The attorney general resolved to do something about this, and managed to get Congress to appropriate money for one full-time clerk's salary, stationery, and office expenses. In addition, he attempted to systematize and preserve the records of his office. Wirt introduced the use of letter-books, in which all correspondence to and from the attorney general was recorded and which provided for the eventual organization and publication of all official opinions given by his office. Although Congress had mandated that the attorneys general live in Washington, he continued to follow the example of his predecessors by maintaining a private legal practice.

Wirt's organizational efforts were not matched by any real effort to increase the duties and responsibilities of the office.

Several congressional statutes did add to the duties of the attorney general during these years, but these tended to follow the 1789 act's mandate of "advice and opinion." For example, the attorney general was required to advise treaty commissioners in their negotiations and validate titles to lands purchased by the government. Yet one crucial organizational weakness remained unchanged. Attorneys general continued to have little or no supervisory authority over the district attorneys and other local federal officials. Indeed, in 1815 Congress created the position of "agent" in the Treasury Department. This agent was responsible for overseeing the activities of federal district attorneys, particularly in matters involving the collection of money or property in the name of the United States government. Since there were few federal criminal statutes at the time, this arrangement was not entirely illogical. Wirt himself admitted that local attorneys didn't really need his supervision, since they were required to be "learned in the law" and could presumably decide what cases to bring and how to bring them on their own. In 1830 Congress replaced Treasury's "agent" with a "Solicitor of the Treasury" and gave the solicitor responsibility for directing district attorneys, marshals, and other local federal officers in *all* matters in which the United States had an interest. While the relationship between the attorney general and the solicitor was generally "amicable," it was also the case that the legal business of the federal government on the local level was in the hands of an official other than the chief legal officer of the country. As a result, district attorneys and marshals developed their own tradition of local independence from any centralized control from Washington. This tradition continued even after direct control was given to the attorney general after 1870.

At least one of Wirt's successors recognized this problem. After his appointment by President Franklin Pierce in 1853, Caleb Cushing prepared a report on the current status of his office and the steps he saw as necessary to make the office equal to other executive and cabinet departments. He explained that through "piecemeal" legislation since 1789 Congress had virtually made the attorney general "the administrative head, under the President, of the legal business of the government," without any formal recognition of this status. Cushing believed that the position was a full-time one. He settled permanently in Washington and became the first attorney general not to engage in outside legal work during his term. Congress encouraged this change by increasing the attorney general's salary to four thousand dollars, on a par with other cabinet officers. Aside from wanting his office to be required to submit "periodic" reports to Congress, Cushing's specific proposals for administrative parity echoed Congress's: adding additional responsibilities to the office, such as granting pardons and being in charge of judicial "commissions." However, he did argue that the attorney general should be responsible for prosecuting all suits in which the United States was involved, even if the government was not an actual party to the suit.

While Cushing considered himself the administrative head of the federal government's legal business, he opposed involving his office in what he considered to be questions of "public policy and executive determination." Responding to a request by Secretary of War Jefferson Davis for a legal opinion as to whether or not some property seized by the city of Kenosha, Wisconsin, might be recovered by the government, Cushing explained that the attorney general had no authority to decide whether the government should act. "The relation of the Attorney General to any one of the Executive Departments, in such questions," he wrote, "is that of counsel to client, to give advice as to the legal right, and instruct procedure, if desired." The attorney general could determine if the government had the right to recover the land, and the procedures to follow, but he could not decide on whether an attempt to recover should be made.

As of 1860 the attorney general's office was not much different from what it had been in 1789. It was still essentially a one-person operation with a small staff and a "slender" budget. The attorney general did not even have a permanent headquarters, and constantly had to move from one department office to another. Most important, other executive departments continued to seek legal counsel from their own legal staffs, and whenever possible, to handle their own legal business. Since district attorneys and marshals were subject to supervision by the solicitor of the Treasury, these officials could expect little help from the attorney general's office. When asked for such assistance, the attorney general simply referred the person to other departments for instructions. This arrangement worked both ways, since letters to local officials from the attorney general were often returned to Washington unanswered. It was not a system that encouraged effective national law enforcement.

The turning point was the Civil War. The military struggle to preserve the Union strengthened nationalist sentiment and led to a greater acceptance of a level of federal authority and involvement in American life hitherto unthinkable. For example, the Morrill Land-Grant College Act and the creation of the Bureau of Education initiated the presence of the federal government in education. The national government became an important element in generating economic growth through such measures as the Homestead Act, land grants for transportation and communication development, and infrastructure construction. And the creation of a federal pension system provided financial support for veterans and their families, marking the opening steps in the national government's commitment to the welfare of its citizens. The legal business of the U.S. government increased dramatically as well during the Civil War years, especially with the large number of pension, property confiscation, and revenue cases resulting directly from the war. Beginning in 1867 proposals to reform the attorney general's office were introduced to Congress. Debate and a full-scale congressional investigation took three more years. Finally, on June 22, 1870, Congress approved an "Act to Establish a Department of Justice."

The act formally recognized the status of the attorney general's office as an independent cabinet-level department. It reaffirmed almost all of the various duties that Congress had given the attorney general over the previous eighty years, and included some "sweeping" new powers. The department was now responsible for an impressive variety of tasks that included maintaining all federal courthouses and federal court records; approving public building plans; codifying federal statutes; supervising the use and sale of federal lands; promoting public health; handling internal revenue and customs matters; and enforcing all federal criminal and civil regulations regarding Indian affairs, the mails, and immigration and naturalization. The size of the attorney general's office increased as well. There would now be two assistant attorneys general and a "solicitor general." The primary function of the solicitor general would be to present oral arguments before the Supreme Court in cases involving the federal government, a function previously given to the attorney general. However, in cases of particular importance or interest the attorney general could still choose to appear before the Court himself. The solicitor general could also handle the day-to-day operations of the Justice Department in the absence of the attorney general. Salaries of all department officers were set, and in a number of instances increased. It was also directed that space be made available in the Treasury building for offices to house the new department. The attorney general was also required to submit an annual report to Congress detailing the department's work, including crimes committed and prosecuted "under the laws of the United States."

By far the most important new responsibility given to the department and the attorney general was direct supervisory authority over district attorneys and their offices throughout the country. This authority was not confined to just legal matters, but extended to other aspects of running local federal offices and courts as well, especially their finances. Yet while the organizational structure was new, the jurisdictional boundaries of department officials in the states continued to be based on the pattern first created under the Judiciary Act of 1789. The lowest level of the federal court system was the district court. Each district had one district attorney and one federal marshal. Depending on the size and importance of the district, many districts also had one assistant district attorney and at least one deputy marshal. All southern states had two federal districts, except Tennessee and Alabama, which had three. The next, or middle, level of the federal court system was the circuit court, which covered two or more states. The Fifth Judicial Circuit Court included Texas, Louisiana, Mississippi, Alabama, Georgia, and Florida. Kentucky was part of the Sixth Circuit, along with Tennessee, Ohio, and Michigan. Virginia, the Carolinas, West Virginia, and Maryland made up the Fourth Circuit.

Thus, in theory at least, there existed by 1871 both the enforcement machinery and the necessary laws to protect the civil and political rights of southern freedmen from increasing white resistance and terror. President Grant, while no believer in racial equality, had supported the extension of voting rights to the freedmen and was committed to the use of federal authority to carry through Republican Reconstruction policies. When Congress created the department in June of 1870, shortly after the first Enforcement Act was passed, President Grant took the opportunity to demand the resignation of Attorney General Ebenezer Hoar, appointing Amos Tappan Akerman to be the first attorney general of the new department. Akerman had two important assets: he was committed to the policy of active federal implementation of Reconstruction rights guarantees, and he was a southerner. Born and educated in New England, Akerman had moved to the South before the Civil War. There he studied law with former attorney general John M. Berrien. During the war Akerman served briefly in the Confederate government, but afterward he became an ardent Republican and was appointed a federal district attorney in Georgia. There he earned a reputation as a strong party advocate and an equally strong supporter of civil rights protection. He brought a number of cases under the Civil Rights Act of 1866 and participated in the drafting of the Georgia state constitution that enfranchised blacks in 1868. He endorsed the extension of voting rights to the freedmen through the Fifteenth Amendment. He recognized, however, that many white southerners opposed it "on account of the supposed ignorance of the class to be enfranchised," but added that "if ignorance did not disqualify white men it should not disqualify black men." It was indicative of the state of the department that when Akerman arrived in Washington to assume his duties he discovered that his staff was housed in three different locations. Akerman and his clerks were in the Treasury Building, opposite the White House; one of the assistant attorneys general was housed in the basement of the Capitol; and the solicitor general, Benjamin H. Bristow of Kentucky, and the other assistant attorneys general and their clerks were in rented office space elsewhere.

Despite the administrative challenges facing Akerman, the new attorney general came to office determined to enforce Republican policies in the South. He was particularly intent on combating the activities of the Ku Klux Klan. Early in his tenure he even traveled to the Carolinas to personally investigate the widespread campaign of Klan terror and intimidation going on in these states. Appalled by the violence there, he declared "that any large portion of our people should be so ensavaged as to perpetrate or excuse such actions is the darkest blot on Southern character in this age." He predicted that only "a desperate contest with bad men" would prevent the Klan and its supporters from wreaking havoc in the South. But promising support was different from actually providing it. Although Congress had voted a supplemental appropriation of fifty thousand dollars for the department to hire detectives to seek out violations of the Enforcement Acts, much of Akerman's knowledge of alleged violations of the acts came from reports by district attorneys in the South and from scores of personal letters sent directly by private citizens to Washington. These detailed a wide variety of crimes, from the "flogging" of a young black man for simply leaving his job to an Alabama man's seeking government protection from the Klan not just because of his political activities but because he had also gotten "into a difficulty with a young Woman, my wife's sister, and we had taken a little flight at her suggestion."

From June of 1870 onward, Enforcement Acts prosecutions were brought by district attorneys throughout the South. By far the largest number of cases—almost two thousand—were initiated during the first three years. And while cases were brought in all southern states, almost half were in two places: the Northern District of Mississippi and South Carolina. Nearly all of the cases were prosecuted under the May 1870 act. Although neither the

Reese nor the *Cruikshank* case originated in Mississippi or South Carolina, the record of these two states illustrates both the successes and failures of the early attempts at national law enforcement. Crucial to effective enforcement efforts were the abilities and efforts of the local Justice Department officials. Because district attorneys and marshals were federal appointees, almost all southern officials in 1870 were Republicans, and a good number of them qualified as carpetbaggers. South Carolina federal district attorney David T. Corbin had been an attorney in New England before serving in the Union army. After the war, and prior to his appointment as district attorney, as an agent for the Freedman's Bureau he became intimately familiar with the perils of freedom experienced by blacks in the state. The bureau was the federal program set up after the war to assist in the education and economic plight of the newly freed slaves. Mississippi federal district attorney G. Wiley Wells was likewise a staunch Republican born in the North. Both men, and most other federal officials at the time, were strong supporters of the congressional Reconstruction agenda. They generally had few doubts about either the necessity or the appropriateness of the legislation they were directed to enforce. District attorneys in the South often went beyond the specific requirements of their situation to bring about more effective enforcement. In South Carolina, District Attorney Corbin brought cases against the Klan for attacks on women and children, even though neither were voters under the protection of the Fifteenth Amendment. Wells, a self-styled "swashbuckler," accompanied his marshals in the chase and capture of prisoners. He gained national notoriety for having a photograph made of captured Klansmen in their disguises and sending a copy to one of the most widely circulating magazines of the era, *Harper's Weekly*. In publishing the picture, the journal helped counter the argument being made by southerners at the time that the Klan was nothing but a figment of northern imaginations.

Equally important to successful Enforcement Acts prosecutions in the South was the direction and assistance provided by the attorney general and the federal government. Obviously, it helped to have an attorney general who supported Congress's

Reconstruction program and the intent of the Fifteenth Amendment and the enforcement legislation. As described above, Attorney General Amos Akerman was committed to the protection of African Americans' rights, and was a vociferous foe of the KKK. His successor in 1872, George H. Williams, would prove far less committed to such protections.

One crucial form of assistance by the government to local officials was federal troops. As of 1870 federal troops remained stationed throughout the South. Enforcement Acts prosecutions often involved indictments of numerous defendants who lived in places distant from the federal court, in communities that probably supported the defendants' activities or were certainly hostile to outside federal authority. A federal marshal, even with a contingent of deputies, could at best expect a defiant and uncooperative population. At worst he might meet armed resistance. Federal troops were authorized to support Justice Department efforts in both northern Mississippi and South Carolina, but with one crucial difference. Under the provisions of the Enforcement Acts federal troops could be used to actually make arrests only when the president formally suspended the writ of habeas corpus. In South Carolina Grant did so, and within a matter of weeks hundreds of suspects were arrested by federal department officials and U.S. troops. In northern Mississippi troops could be used only to escort marshals and their deputies. Even here problems arose, since most often the army provided infantry units rather than the faster and more mobile cavalry. As one soldier explained it, "[I]nfantry could not move two miles before the cry 'Yankees are coming,' giving of course ample time for the wicked to flee."

The availability of financial resources for local officials also proved critical to early enforcement efforts. The Justice Department in Washington was bombarded daily with requests from district attorneys for additional funds, for everything from buying office supplies to hiring additional deputy marshals and prosecuting attorneys. In one of the bureaucratic snags that would not be worked out until the 1880s, the congressional budget cycle for executive departments did not coincide with the federal judicial schedule. As a result, even fiscally responsible district attorneys found themselves out of money in the middle of court proceedings, especially if the sessions extended into the summer months. Moreover, the department had no formal accounting system, either in Washington or in its field offices. One southern district attorney was reputed to have kept all his office financial records in a (one hopes unused) spittoon. Local officials simply sent in requests for additional funds as needed, and since Washington had no regular procedure for tracking such expenses, it responded in a similarly haphazard fashion. Some requests would be granted, others would be turned down. Occasionally, the attorney general would admonish individual district attorneys and marshals to consider ways of "reducing expenditures." Or the attorney general would send out what were known as "Circular Letters" to all local officials, directing them to incur expenses "as shall be absolutely necessary."

Even more problematic to effective law enforcement was the way department officials outside of Washington were compensated. Prior to 1870 all local officials were under a "fee system," by which they were paid a specified sum for each case brought. The unfairness of this system was obvious. Some officials brought "petty and frivolous proceedings" to increase their fees. Other officials ended up impoverished, either because they were too honest to bring unnecessary cases or because they happened to work in either sparsely populated or exceptionally law-abiding districts. Others did well. While serving as a district attorney in 1817, future attorney general William Wirt reported that in a single day he had managed to win several judgments for the government. He ended up earning almost two hundred dollars in fees, a substantial sum in those days. "To-morrow," he wrote happily, "I go on again in the same way."

The 1870 legislation creating the Justice Department made no attempt to change this system, except to place some limits on the amount of fees that could be generated. Even so, the consequences of having government attorneys receiving far less than their opposing counsel was clearly recognized by Attorney General Akerman. In his first annual report to Congress Akerman complained that "[t]he present system has a natural tendency to diminish the zeal of the officer, when his maximum is reached, and to tempt him to seek improper incidental expenses." It was not uncommon, noted Akerman's successor, George H. Williams, to find district attorneys receiving fifty dollars for a case while their opposing counsel was being paid in the thousands of dollars. Despite these complaints, and the recognition of the harm done to morale and the image of the department, this fee system was not abolished until 1893. Under such circumstances, it was understandable how many southerners viewed the multiple cases brought under the Enforcement Acts as primarily a way for federal officials to make money.

Along with these internal problems federal officials faced white southerners' open and widespread resistance and opposition to enforcement efforts. In many instances, even where violence and murder was involved, the alleged perpetrators were viewed as heroes by their families and communities. As such they could expect all kinds of assistance and support. "Spotters" would regularly warn those for whom warrants had been issued of the approach of marshals and their deputies. In some places local Justice Department officials were forced to communicate by the far slower mails because telegraph offices were in Democratic hands. Once captured, defendants might even expect crowds to appear in a show of communal support. On their return from court proceedings they were treated not as indicted or convicted felons but as "the victims of villainous subordination" or the "unfortunate people" who themselves had been "kidnaped" from their homes and families. Some communities went so far as to hold contests and concerts to raise money for the defense of those accused of violating the Enforcement Acts, or to pay the fines imposed for men convicted for doing so. In one instance the people of Aberdeen, Mississippi, reimbursed a local blacksmith for the cost of a whip and his fine following his conviction for administering two hundred lashes to a black man accused of being "uppity."

White southerners also made sure the men accused of violating the election laws were given the best legal counsel available. Ironically, this could even include hiring the same northern "car-

{ *Reconstruction and Black Suffrage* }

petbagger" attorneys working for the federal government. In South Carolina, where hundreds of indictments were brought against the Klan, a public subscription campaign was organized by ex-Confederate leader and future governor Wade Hampton to create a defense fund for those accused. The money raised was used to hire two former attorneys general, U.S. senator Reverdy Johnson of Maryland and Henry Stanbery of Ohio. Their defense work in South Carolina would not be their last appearance in opposition to the Enforcement Acts. Johnson would be part of the defense team in Louisiana in the *Cruikshank* case, and Stanbery would appear for the defendants in Kentucky in *Reese*.

Such opposition was clearly worrisome and frustrating, but of even greater concern was the willingness of Democrats and those opposed to the Enforcement Acts to resort to intimidation and actual violence against federal officials and all those who cooperated with them. Since those accused of committing violations of the election laws were seen as heroes and even victims themselves, it is not surprising that those who brought prosecutions were seen as the real villains. Even federal officials who were native southerners found themselves treated with the same suspicion and hostility as more recent arrivals. District attorneys, marshals and their deputies, and special prosecuting attorneys brought in to assist in Enforcement Acts prosecutions were constantly harassed and threatened. Their character and motives were under constant scrutiny and attack by the Democratic press. Because in the South in the late nineteenth century reputation mattered enormously, such tactics could be as effective as actual physical assaults. And those occurred as well. Mississippi federal district attorney Wells was alleged to have received a "dose of poison" during the prosecutions in that state.

The campaign of harassment and intimidation extended to witnesses and jurors as well. Persons scheduled to testify were suddenly called away on some unspecified "personal" business. Those who did testify could expect all sorts of retribution, as could jurors who returned guilty verdicts. Indeed, juries were a particular problem for federal prosecutors, since jury rolls were taken from voter registration lists. During these early years the lists still contained large numbers of white Democratic voters, and therefore the juries in enforcement cases invariably contained one or more members who were less than impartial. In reply to the attorney general's query as to his lack of success in obtaining any convictions in his district despite the massive evidence and support he had received in the prosecutions, one southern district attorney noted succinctly, if profanely, that it was due to the fact that the juries in his district were all "fucked."

Under these circumstances what was remarkable was the number and extent of successful prosecutions during the two years immediately following passage of the various Enforcement Acts. The largest number of successful prosecutions was brought in South Carolina and northern Mississippi, yet even in these states it was unclear exactly what had been accomplished. Moreover, by late 1872 a number of factors already had begun casting uncertainty on the future of the government's enforcement program. Dissatisfied with President Grant's administration and policies, members of his party had begun organizing their own independent or "liberal" faction within the Republican Party. These "Liberal Republicans" included a number of early supporters of the Fifteenth Amendment and the enforcement legislation, such as Carl Schurz and Charles Sumner. These individuals now seemed to have reservations about the federal government's role in implementing its promise to the freedpeople. The liberal agenda placed cleaning up government corruption above enforcement of federal protections for African Americans in the South. Much as did former president Johnson, they saw the states as having the ultimate responsibility for deciding who could or could not vote, and they believed that the greater the federal government's role in the electoral process, the greater the chances for the abuse and corruption that they so despised.

In spite of this opposition Grant received the Republican nomination for reelection, and in the November 1872 contest won a landslide victory. His unequivocal support for continued federal protection of civil and political rights appealed to the majority of the Republican Party's northern constituency, and certainly accounted for his victories in six southern states, where African-

American votes again proved crucial. But the seeds for some sort of retreat had been sown. Economic and political troubles after 1873 cost Grant even more support within his party and led to a Democratic resurgence. More moderate Republicans began to voice doubts about the practical and constitutional limits of the national government's role in protecting blacks in the South. The political winds that had brought the Fifteenth Amendment and the Enforcement Acts were beginning to die down.

Another factor that led to the increasing uncertainty over suffrage protections was the appointment of a new attorney general in 1871. Attorney General Amos Akerman had demonstrated his commitment to implementing the Enforcement Acts, and initiated and supported the mass of early prosecutions. Although he did not participate in the actual trials, his personal involvement in the South Carolina Klan prosecutions reflected his hatred for the organization. He made no secret of his intent to destroy the Invisible Empire. But what he saw as a moral imperative, others in the Grant administration saw as an "obsession." Moreover, he questioned prevailing strategy that justified protecting black voting rights for partisan purposes, believing that southern blacks should be able to vote for the best candidates no matter what their party. The final straw came when he issued a series of opinions hostile to two of Grant's wealthiest supporters, railroad magnates Collis P. Huntington and Jay Gould. Akerman was forced to resign on December 12, 1871. He believed that northerners were becoming less concerned with the atrocities that continued to plague the South than they were with a "progress (that) runs away from the past."

Two days later Grant appointed George H. Williams as the new attorney general. Williams had been born in New York in 1820, and was admitted to the bar there after reading the law. He served for a time as a state judge in Iowa in the 1840s, and in 1853 was appointed by President Franklin Pierce to be chief justice of the Oregon Territorial Court. In 1864 he was elected Republican senator from the new state of Oregon. During the early part of Reconstruction he earned his Radical credentials through his work on the Joint Committee on Reconstruction. Williams claimed authorship of the Reconstruction Act of 1867, and introduced the Tenure of Office Act, which became the basis for President Andrew Johnson's impeachment. Williams was not reelected for a second term, but in 1871 Grant appointed him to a special commission negotiating with Great Britain to resolve claims arising from British actions during the Civil War. His appointment as attorney general in December 1871 seemed at first to bode well for the Justice Department's enforcement efforts. But it soon became evident that this was not to be. Williams's primary interest seemed more advancement of his own career than a real commitment to his constitutional responsibilities, an interest sustained by an evidently ambitious and "exceedingly costly" wife. In 1873 Grant, however, nominated Williams to be chief justice of the Supreme Court. Ironically, the nomination was withdrawn after a Senate investigation discovered that Williams had removed a federal district attorney in Oregon who was about to prosecute Senator John H. Mitchell, a political ally of the attorney general, for election fraud under the Enforcement Acts. Added to this were charges that Williams and his wife had used Justice Department funds for the purchase of a "landaulet" luxury carriage and the hiring of liveried servants for his household. There were even reports that Mrs. Williams had saved a number of individuals from prosecution in exchange for money. Although he remained as attorney general until 1875, the future of federal rights protection in the South was unclear while "Landaulet Williams" served as the nation's chief law enforcement officer.

Underlying all these various problems with the implementation of the Enforcement Act in the southern states was the question that had bothered some Republicans, and almost all Democrats, during the original debates over the measures. How would the judiciary view the legislation? Section 2 of the Fifteenth Amendment authorized Congress to pass "appropriate" legislation to enforce the provisions of the amendment. But what constituted "appropriate" would ultimately be a matter for the federal courts to decide. Ever since *Marbury v. Madison* in 1803 the Supreme Court had the authority to determine the constitutionality of acts of Congress. Admittedly, up until 1872 the Supreme Court had used that authority sparingly in striking *down* federal legislation. A number of early lower federal court rulings in 1870 and 1871 suggested judicial support for the enforcement legislation. But the ultimate repository of judicial review was the United States Supreme Court, and in 1872 the Court had not yet ruled on a case involving the actual meaning and substance of the acts. Three cases growing out of the South Carolina Klan trials had been filed with the Supreme Court, but one, *U.S. v. Sapaugh*, was blocked from hearing by incoming attorney general Williams, and the other two, *U.S. v. Avery* and *Ex parte Greer*, were essentially decided on procedural grounds.

Under these circumstances most everyone agreed that only a Supreme Court ruling could clear up any uncertainty about the constitutionality of the Enforcement Acts and the government's entire enforcement policy. Since the crimes enumerated in the acts were still being perpetrated, local Justice Department officials were eager for guidance from the Supreme Court, particularly since they weren't getting much from within the department hierarchy. Republicans, including the Enforcement Act's supporters, now looked to the Supreme Court for vindication, or more cynically, an excuse to cover a "retreat" from their harsher Reconstruction initiatives. But most of all, Democratic politicians and lawyers looked to the Court for what Henry Stanbery called "the true construction of the Constitution." What opponents and supporters of the laws needed were prosecutions that could be used as test cases, that would present the constitutional issues both clearly and in such a way as to get them past the lower federal courts and up to the Supreme Court.

Two cases presented themselves, although neither came from the hotbeds of enforcement prosecutions. In January 1873, a black man by the name of William Garner was denied the right to vote in a Lexington, Kentucky, municipal election for his alleged failure to pay a $1.50 tax. And three months after that, on April 13, Easter Sunday, scores of Louisiana blacks were brutally massacred in one of the most horrific single instances of violence of the Reconstruction era. That the bloodshed took place in a Louisiana parish named for the incumbent President Grant did not go unnoticed.

CHAPTER 3

Massacre at Colfax Courthouse

Even during a time of widespread violence against African Americans, the murder of over one hundred black men at the Colfax Courthouse in Grant Parish, Louisiana, on Easter Sunday 1873 stands out as one of the most heinous single instances of racial terror in post–Civil War America. If nothing else it demonstrated white southern Democrats' zero tolerance for their former slaves holding even the barest of political power. Variously described at the time as an "outrage," a "riot," a "massacre," and a "battle," the event showed Democrats' willingness, if not eagerness, to murder to get that power back. It also highlighted the simple fact that race was the fundamental "fault line" in the complicated and contentious Louisiana politics at the time. William Cruikshank's and his fellow defendants' prosecution and conviction for the murders on Easter Sunday 1873 became an important test of the federal government's enforcement policies. The Supreme Court's ruling on those convictions three years later would be seen as signaling a "retreat" from those same enforcement policies.

Reconstruction in Louisiana was indeed complex, and in its own way as bitter and violent as anywhere else in the South. Part of the reason for this was that Reconstruction began even before the Civil War had ended. Following the occupation of New Orleans by Union troops in April 1862, President Lincoln began the process of restoring the state back into the Union. Underlying Lincoln's plans was the presence of a substantial number of white Unionists who had opposed secession. Unfortunately, factionalism and corruption within the Unionists' ranks, as well as their ambivalence about emancipation and black rights, doomed these efforts. At the same time, New Orleans was home to a large population of educated and vocal free blacks, a good number of whom served with the federal forces occupying the city. This group became the vanguard for demanding enfranchisement and political equality. Aside from emancipation and the most limited of suffrage rights, Louisiana blacks were generally ignored during President Johnson's Reconstruction program. The low point came in the summer of 1866, when a politically motivated race riot in New Orleans left almost fifty African Americans dead. It was only following congressional Reconstruction that Louisiana adopted a new constitution (at a convention that included a majority of African-American delegates) that enfranchised Louisiana blacks.

The new Republican regime that came to power in 1867 was beset with internal discord and increasingly organized Democratic opposition. Governor Henry C. Warmoth, a carpetbagger, proved unable to either maintain party unity or stem the wave of Democratic violence against Republicans of both races across the state. Although African-American voters provided the key to Republican electoral success, Warmoth pointedly ignored their leaders' claims to patronage and real political power. Prevented by law from seeking reelection, in 1872 Warmoth and his supporters bolted the Republican Party and joined a Fusion ticket with Democrats, who then made Warmoth their candidate for U.S. senator. The Fusionists ran John D. McEnery for governor, while the Republican candidate was another carpetbagger, William Pitt Kellogg.

Even by Louisiana's notoriously low standards the state elections of 1872 were what one commentator described as a "fiasco." Both Republicans and Fusionists claimed victory in the statewide offices, and in fact no one would ever know which side really won. On January 13, 1873, Louisianans had the unique opportunity to witness two sets of state governments inaugurated in New Orleans. The rival Republican Kellogg's and Fusionist McEnery's administrations and supporters both claimed to be the legitimate authority in the state. Aside from supportive telegrams to Kellogg from Washington, President Grant and Attorney General Williams were reluctant to become directly involved in the mess. For his part, Kellogg seemed ambivalent about such support, probably believing that he had the upper hand. In fact, by the end of February Kellogg had managed to solidify his authority in New Orleans. In large part this was due to the presence of federal troops in the city. But resistance to Kellogg and the Republicans by Fusionists and Democrats broke out elsewhere in the state, far from state and federal authorities in New Orleans. One of those places was Grant Parish.

Located along the Red River, about three hundred fifty miles north of New Orleans, Grant Parish (a "parish" in Louisiana is the equivalent of a county in other states) had not even existed prior to 1868. That year a wealthy Republican planter and state legislator, William Calhoun, convinced the legislature to carve out a new parish from two existing ones and to locate the parish courthouse in a one-story brick building that had formerly served as Calhoun's stable. To Democrats in the area the new parish was doubly provocative. It was deliberately named after the incumbent president and former commander of the Union armies, Ulysses S. Grant, and the parish seat was named for Grant's vice president, Schuyler Colfax. Even more abhorrent to Democrats was the fact that the parish lines were drawn in such a way as to make African Americans a slight but critical majority of the population. As in most of its near neighbors in the region, the parish's Democrats included a Klan organization, the Knights of the White Camelia. The Knights were dedicated to the supremacy of the white race. The idea of blacks voting, let alone holding political power, was anathema to them. The organization called openly for a race war against the "Black Devils," a war that would rid whites of the "black vulture."

Not surprisingly, there had been trouble in Grant Parish even before 1872. Local Republicans were regularly harassed, and in September 1871 a mob set fire to a house shared by two former Republican officeholders, William Philips and Delos White. Both men were white but had been strong supporters of black rights. As they attempted to escape the burning house, White was shot dead. What complicated the situation was the presence of Republicans, including parish sheriff Alfred Shelby and his deputy Columbus Christopher Nash, among the attackers. As elsewhere in the state, Republicans in the Grant Parish were becoming increasingly split along racial lines. Conservative white Republicans who thought of themselves as the "better sort" supported black voting rights in principle, but became far less enthusiastic when blacks actually held office and either demanded or exercised real authority. Indeed, there was often little difference between white Republicans and their Democratic counterparts when their racial supremacy was challenged. Phillips and White had been targeted because of their open support for a group of militant "black carpetbaggers." Many of these black men, like their leader William Ward, were Union army veterans. Some had served with federal troops in New Orleans before moving to the region. They refused to remain passive in the face of intimidation and opposition to their rights. Ward, described as "brave and determined" by his supporters and a "troublemaker" by his enemies, had been appointed by Governor Warmoth to lead and train the local militia. What was intended to be a biracial unit, a demonstration of Republican racial harmony, became under Ward's captaincy an all-black company. The company began assisting local federal authorities in combating Klan violence, thus further heightening racial tensions in the area.

Following Delos White's murder, Phillips, along with Ward and his militia, attempted unsuccessfully to bring the perpetrators to justice. In the summer of 1872 the refusal of a federal grand jury to indict those responsible, particularly Shelby and Nash, completed the polarization of Grant Parish politics along racial lines. With the exception of a few white supporters, blacks in the parish were now politically on their own as the November 1872 elections approached. Although he escaped indictment, Columbus C. Nash ran for parish sheriff as the "martyred" candidate of the Fusionist Party. His attorney, Alphonse Cazabat, ran for local judge, and their candidate for parish recorder was James Hadnot, a local Democratic planter and reputed Knights of the White Camelia leader. The Republican ticket included an African-American candidate, R. C. Register, for sheriff and Daniel Shaw, a white man, for judge.

The outcome of the 1872 contest in Grant Parish, as in the rest of the state, was inconclusive. Both sides claimed victory. Governor Warmoth, serving out the last weeks of his term, commissioned the Fusionist candidates for all parish offices. In early January Nash, Cazabat, and Hadnot took possession of the parish courthouse in Colfax and began carrying out their duties. As Governor Kellogg and his Republican administration became more firmly entrenched in power, the Fusionist officials of the parish sent two former Republican attorneys to New Orleans to seek confirmation of their positions. Kellogg appeared to be willing at first to recognize the Fusionists' control of parish offices. But for reasons that still remain unclear, the governor changed his mind and formally declared Register and Shaw to be the parish's sheriff and judge. Shortly thereafter, a group of blacks, led by Ward, sheriff-elect Register, and judge-elect Shaw, climbed into an open window of the Colfax courthouse and began their occupation of the building.

Whether Register and Shaw actually intended to carry out their newly confirmed positions, or whether their presence in the courthouse was primarily a symbolic act of defiance, is not clear. What is certain is that groups of whites in the parish and the surrounding countryside began mobilizing immediately. Rumors spread among the white population that blacks had initiated a "reign of terror"and that armed units of African-American men roamed the countryside intending to "exterminate" all white people they could find. One incident came to be used by whites to lend credence to these fears. William Rutland was a Republican attorney in Colfax who had joined Nash and Cazabat in bolting the party for the Fusionists in November. He had been one of the emissaries sent to Governor Kellogg back in January to confirm the Fusionist victory. Angered by his treachery, on April 1 a group of blacks forced Rutland and his family from their home and ransacked the building. Although no one was physically harmed, a coffin containing the remains of Rutland's recently drowned young daughter was dumped on the ground, and the body fell out. For whites the incident became yet more evidence of the "rapacious bestiality" and murderous intent of the black population.

In fact, it was the black population that had real cause to fear. As word spread of the various groups of whites organizing to march on Colfax, more blacks, including women and children, began converging on the courthouse for protection. By April 7 some four hundred freedpersons were camped out around the Colfax courthouse. Ironically, the courthouse was probably one of the least safe places to be. It was small and relatively isolated from surrounding buildings, and there was no natural cover for defensive purposes. A number of the black defenders, mostly those from Ward's militia unit, were armed with shotguns and rifles. In addition, two primitive cannons were fashioned out of discarded pipes, and a rude earthen and wooden-plank breastworks was constructed in a semicircle around the courthouse. The weakness of such preparations was evident. Terrified local white Republicans, including Daniel Shaw, one of the original occupiers of the building, slipped quietly away.

During the first days of April there were a number of encounters in the surrounding countryside between the white forces converging on Colfax and the defenders. None resulted in bloodshed. Then on April 5, a special deputy from a nearby community, J. R. Payne, attempted to ease the growing crisis by negotiating a truce with Ward and several of the other defenders. While negotiations were going on word reached this group that a force of whites marching toward Colfax had come upon a black farmer named Jesse McKinney, who happened to be innocently mending his fence at the time, and shot him dead. Certain now that the white forces gathering at Colfax were not interested in any compromise, Ward and his followers returned to the courthouse to prepare for the inevitable confrontation. Several days after this incident Ward, realizing how desperate the situation was for those at the courthouse, left for New Orleans to seek help from the federal authorities. One of Ward's militiamen, Levin Allen, was placed in charge of the defenders.

The fighting at Colfax Courthouse began shortly after noon on Easter Sunday, April 13, 1873. By that time the number of whites besieging the courthouse stood at over three hundred armed men. Their commander was none other than erstwhile sheriff Columbus C. Nash. Nash began by ordering those occupying the courthouse to leave. When that order was ignored, he then gave the women and children camped out around the building thirty minutes to leave. Once they had left the shooting began, although no one could say for sure who fired the first shot. For the next several hours the defenders of the courthouse, shooting mainly from behind their breastworks, exchanged fire with Nash's men. Neither side suffered any serious casualties. A group of Nash's men then managed to maneuver a small cannon they had taken off a nearby Red River steamboat to a gap they had discovered in the defenders' fortifications. Now they fired at the defenders from behind, but that too proved ineffective in dislodging Allen's men. Changing tactics, another group of whites now charged through an opening in the breastworks behind the courthouse.

The defenders panicked. About sixty men quickly retreated back inside the courthouse building. Others ran toward the nearby river and woods. Many of the besiegers gave chase and slaughtered those they caught on the spot. Meanwhile, the rest of Nash's forces turned their attention to the courthouse. After an exchange of gunfire with the men inside the building, an elderly black man captured early on was persuaded, on promise of his own safety, to crawl up to the building with a torch and set the roof on fire. Firing from both sides resumed as the building began to burn. Two white flags, one made from a torn shirt and the other a page from a book, appeared in the courthouse windows. The shooting stopped. The whites approached the building and called for all those inside to put down their weapons and come out. As those inside began running out, two of the besiegers heading toward the building were suddenly shot down. White witnesses later claimed that the two men had been shot by those defenders still inside the building on account of their "undying hatred for the white race." The evidence, however, suggested that at least one of the men was a victim of "friendly fire." An autopsy revealed a fatal bullet wound in the man's back which, a later investigator concluded, meant that if he had been shot by those inside the courthouse "he must have been running backwards towards the building." Infuriated, Nash's men now began the wholesale massacre of the defenders fleeing the building. Many were "ridden down in the open fields and shot without mercy" by those whites on horseback. Most of the bodies later recovered were found unarmed. Some of the bodies of those slaughtered were either hidden or dumped into the Red River. A number of the recovered bodies of the victims were horribly mutilated. By four o'clock the "battle" was over, but not the killing.

That evening about fifty of the black defenders who had thus far managed to survive the massacre remained as prisoners. They were held by a small contingent of Nash's men who had not already headed back to their homes. Around eight o'clock Nash himself visited the prisoners and promised that they would all be freed the next morning. After he left, the prisoners were marched off in a line of pairs, supposedly to be taken to a nearby jail for the night. But as they proceeded along the by-then darkened road, the prisoners were separated and executed. One participant later described it this way: "I heard Luke Hadnot say, 'I can take five,' and five men stepped out. Luke lined them up and his old gun went off, and he killed all five of them with two shots. Then it was like popcorn in a skillet. They killed those forty-eight." Miraculously, at least one of the prisoners survived. An elderly freedman, Benjamin Brimm, was shot once through the head, and when it appeared he was still alive, he was shot again through the back. Somehow, Brimm managed to crawl away and avoid detection while the killing went on. He survived and later became one of the government's chief witnesses before the federal grand jury that indicted those responsible for the massacre.

The following day police and federal troops from New Orleans began arriving in Grant Parish, along with a deputy U.S. marshal. But it was clearly too late. As one New Orleans newspaper succinctly proclaimed: "The Whites have retaken Colfax, and there is not a Negro to be found for miles around." The estimate of the number of victims varied widely depending on who was doing the counting and when, ranging from as low as 50 to over 400. A later investigation of the scene by army officials concluded that about 105 black men were killed, but acknowledged that numbers of bodies had been hidden or removed, or dumped into the Red River, and would never be found. Regardless of the actual number of men killed, the perpetrators would only be charged with the murder of one person. As might be expected, those responsible for these deaths had quickly fled the scene. In the weeks following Easter Sunday, various government forces unsuccessfully tried to round up and arrest all those involved. One of the "ringleaders," C. C. Nash, supposedly escaped by swimming across the Red River on his horse under a hail of bullets from a government posse. Most disappeared back to the anonymity of their homes and families. Some fled as far as Texas, never to return to Louisiana. Ultimately, officials arrested nine men and brought them back to New Orleans to stand trial. Included in that group was the heretofore unknown participant named William J. Cruikshank.

Even at a time when attacks on blacks in the South were almost routine, the events in Grant Parish could not be ignored in the press. While New Orleans newspapers, and those elsewhere in the South, talked about a "battle," the northern press called it what it was, a "massacre" and an "outrage." Even Attorney General Williams, who had already demonstrated his less than zealous concern for implementing the Enforcement Acts, directed the federal attorney in New Orleans, James R. Beckwith, to begin an immediate investigation and prosecution of those responsible and to "spare no pains or expense" in the process. As was increasingly true elsewhere in the South, the problem in this case was the large number of persons involved and the resources necessary to enforce the federal statutes. When it became evident that neither the funds nor the personnel needed would be available, Williams directed the district attorney to focus on prosecuting a smaller group of the ringleaders.

At the time of the events in Grant Parish the federal circuit court in New Orleans was already in session for its regular spring term. Presiding was District Court Judge Edward H. Durrell. On June 10, 1873, fifteen grand jurors were empaneled to hear the charges brought by District Attorney Beckwith, based on his investigations. Their responsibility was to hear the evidence brought by the district attorney and determine if there was sufficient evidence to indict anyone. The jury's foreman was an African American, Charles S. Sauvinet, who had already gained notoriety as a rights activist by successfully suing a barkeeper for refusing to serve him. After deliberating for six days the grand jury indicted Columbus C. Nash, William Cruikshank, William H. Hadnot, and ninety-five other named individuals "for banding and conspiring together with the purpose and intent to prevent and hinder citizens of the United States, in the full exercise and enjoyment of the rights and privileges guaranteed or secured to them by the Constitution and laws of the United States; and for wilful murder while so conspiring and banded."

The indictment ran to over 150 handwritten pages, and was "a jungle of a document." One reason for its unusual length was that for each of the thirty-two specific charges, or counts, all ninety-eight defendants' names were listed. Despite his eagerness to prosecute those responsible for this "revolting and horrible" act, it was also likely that the district attorney had difficulty drafting the document and did so hurriedly. Moreover, he must have been aware that Democrats were looking for cases with which to challenge the constitutionality of the Enforcement Acts. In fairness to Beckwith, the circumstances of the case were unusual. For one thing, at least some of those killed had been armed. If all the known dead were named as victims, could that be used by the defense? Despite the large number of men murdered on Easter Sunday, the indictment only specified two victims, Levi Nelson and Alexander Tillman. Nelson, in fact, had survived the massacre and would become a key witness for the government at the trials. Even more problematic were the specific statutory crimes alleged. What constitutionally protected "rights and privileges" of Nelson and Tillman had been violated by the defendants?

All thirty-two counts of the indictment were based on the May 1870 Enforcement Act. The first sixteen counts fell under section 6 of the act. That section made it a crime for two or more persons to "band or conspire together" for the purpose of hindering or depriving anyone from "the free exercise and enjoyment of any right or privilege granted or secured . . . by the Constitution of the laws of the United States." The defendants were charged with banding together "with the unlawful and felonious intent and purpose to deprive, injure, oppress, threaten, and intimidate" Nelson and Tillman and thereby prevent the two from exercising their "lawful" rights. In separate counts, the indictment then specified the rights violated. The three rights came from the Bill of Rights: the right to peaceful assembly (First Amendment); the right to bear arms (Second Amendment); and the right not to be deprived of life, liberty, or property without due process of law (Fifth Amendment). These counts reflected a strategy used by federal attorneys elsewhere in the South in prosecuting Ku Klux Klan outrages, most effectively in the South Carolina Klan trials in 1872. This strategy presumed that ratification of the Fourteenth Amendment had "nationalized" the rights guaranteed in the Bill of Rights. The federal government was now responsible for protecting these rights even when the infringements alleged came from the states or private citizens. From this perspective section 6 of the 1870 Enforcement Act was constitutional under the Fourteenth, as well as the Fifteenth, Amendment. Judge William B. Woods had seemed to suggest as much in an 1871 federal court ruling, *U.S. v. Hall*, upholding the convictions of a group of whites who had fired on a mass meeting of black Republicans in Alabama.

District Attorney Beckwith, however, faced additional concerns. The first was the Supreme Court's recent ruling in the *Slaughterhouse Cases*, coming also out of Louisiana, which seriously questioned any expansive meaning of federally protected rights under the Fourteenth Amendment. However, what transpired at Colfax Courthouse went beyond mere deprivation of "civil" rights. What happened on Easter Sunday was mass murder. Moreover, the black men killed that day were at the scene as the direct result of an election and their exercise of their right to vote. They were killed because they were "of African descent, and persons of color" who had exercised that right to vote, and because they dared attempt to claim the offices and political authority that was legally theirs. Of what use was the franchise if force of arms and murder could overturn its results? The district attorney recognized this, as shown by the fact that the last sixteen counts of the indictment restated the charges previously made, but added to each count the charge of "murder" with respect to Tillman. Finally, the defendants were accused of denying both Nelson and Tillman "the right to vote at any future election, knowing them to be qualified," and intending to "put them in fear of bodily harm, injure, and oppress them, because they had voted at a previous election held in November, 1872." The May 1870 Enforcement Act had, after all, been passed to "enforce the right of citizens of the United States to vote in the several states, and for other purposes." Although the indictment named ninety-eight individuals, only the nine persons taken into custody by federal authorities following the incident actually stood trial. And while the case was docketed as the *United States v. C. C. Nash and others*, Nash remained at large following his escape. The nine men, John P. Hadnot, William Cruikshank, Thomas J. Hickman, Dennis Lemoine, Prudhomme Lemoine, Alfred Lewis, Clement C. Penn, William B. Irwin, and Oscar Givens, were arraigned before Judge Durrell on December 3, 1873. All pled not guilty to the charges. The trial began on February 23, 1874, in New Orleans, but now presiding was Circuit Court Judge William B. Woods, who was joined at times by Judge Durrell. Louisiana Democrats, who believed this case would be an opportunity to test the constitutionality of the Enforcement Act, held a successful public subscription to fund the defense of those accused. The nine were defended by a team of attorneys that included two prominent Democratic lawyers, R. H. Marr and E. John Ellis. Also listed as defendants' counsel were William R. Witaker, H. C. Costellanos, and D. S. Bryan. District Attorney Beckwith appeared for the government. The trial lasted almost two months, with almost three hundred witnesses testifying. After deliberating for nearly six weeks, the jury found one of the defendants, Alfred Lewis, not guilty of all charges. Because the jury was unable to agree on a verdict for the other eight defendants, Judge Woods was forced to declare a mistrial.

On May 18, 1874, a second trial commenced for the remaining eight men. Judge Woods was now joined on the bench by

Associate Supreme Court Justice P. Bradley, who presided for the first several days and then left to attend to his circuit court duties outside Louisiana. For the most part this trial was a repeat of the first, with the same counsel and most of the same witnesses. Reflecting the defense strategy to use this as a test case, Attorney Marr motioned to "strike" or remove several of the counts of the indictment on the grounds that they were unconstitutional. The motion was "held under advisement" by the court until the end of the trial, when and if any of the defendants were found guilty. On June 10, after only two days' deliberation this time, the jury announced its verdict. Cruikshank, Hadnot, and Irwin were found guilty on the first sixteen counts, and not guilty on the other sixteen (that is, the murder charges). The other five defendants were found not guilty on all charges.

Following announcement of the verdict, the attorneys for the three convicted moved unsuccessfully for a new trial. The Court was then asked to consider the earlier motion to strike out all but one of the counts upon which the defendants were found guilty. The defense attorneys now asked for a motion in "arrest of judgement," in effect asking the Court to set aside the guilty verdicts. Attorney Marr argued that the acts charged in the indictment were not "cognizable" under federal law, and were therefore not under the federal court's jurisdiction. He singled out section 6 of the May 1870 Enforcement Act as "not constitutionally within the jurisdiction of the Courts of the United States." Marr contended that the actions committed by the defendants were "judicially cognizable by State Tribunals only, and legislative action therein is among the constitutionally reserved rights of the several states." He also maintained that two of the counts charged were "too vague, general, insufficient and uncertain to afford proper notice to plead and prepare their defense, and set forth no specific offences under the Law." Ironically, this last claim, based on the same federal Bill of Rights (the Fourth and Fifth Amendments in this instance) that Cruikshank's attorneys would argue in their appeal before the Supreme Court, did *not* apply to the states.

By this time Justice Bradley had returned to New Orleans,

and since Bradley and Judge Woods had presided at the trial, both were to rule on the motion. Judge Woods ruled that the charges in the indictment were "good and sufficient" in law and contained matters that were indictable under federal law. He believed the motion to set aside the convictions should be denied. Bradley was of the "contrary opinion," and unlike Woods, stated his reasons at some length. Bradley began by conceding that all three Reconstruction Amendments, the Thirteenth, Fourteenth, and Fifteenth, empowered Congress to pass legislation enforcing the rights extended under the amendments. For example, he noted that the Civil Rights Act of 1866 had been passed to enforce the Thirteenth Amendment's prohibition of involuntary servitude in any state. But such enforcement authority was limited, according to Bradley, in two ways: It was limited by the nature of the right itself and by the relationship between federal and state authority.

Bradley seemed to recognize two types of "rights." One type of right was a simple affirmative right, his example of which was the Thirteenth Amendment. By requiring states to abolish slavery within their boundaries, the amendment created the affirmative right of persons not to be a slave or be treated as one. Congress could pass laws making it a crime for states or individuals to prevent someone from exercising that right. The other type of right was a negative, or "do not infringe," right. The example he used here was the First Amendment, which prohibited Congress from "making any law" denying persons the right, for instance, to peaceably assemble. With this type of right Congress could not pass laws punishing those who attempted to prevent persons from so meeting. That authority, Bradley concluded, rested with the states. That led to his second distinction, the limits of state versus federal authority. Congress had the authority to enforce constitutional provisions, including all amendments. However, "ordinary" crimes, or crimes against the enjoyment of a constitutional right that "spring from ordinary felonious intent," fell under state authority and laws. His list of such "ordinary" crimes included robbery, theft, assaults, and murder.

Bradley's distinctions by themselves were not especially novel, but the linguistic gymnastics he used to apply them to the Fourteenth and Fifteenth Amendments, the Enforcement Act, and the case before him were rather curious. For the justice, both amendments represented the "negative" type of right above. Indeed, both amendments were drafted in the same negative language, "No state shall make or enforce . . ." But they were not really the same! The Fourteenth Amendment was far more limiting of congressional authority because it did not secure the civil rights of citizens directly, but merely prohibited their infringement by the states. Protection of these rights was therefore up to the states themselves. Congress could legislate to provide a "preventive or compensatory remedy" only if and when the states failed to do so. This view of the Fourteenth Amendment's scope was consistent with the Supreme Court's recent ruling in the *Slaughterhouse Cases*. In that case the Court severely narrowed the range of "privileges and immunities" that came under nationally protected rights of citizenship. Justice Bradley in fact had disagreed with the Court's ruling, supporting a nationalistic and activist view of the Fourteenth Amendment's potential.

But Bradley did not apply the same limits on the scope of the Fifteenth Amendment, even though he found them to be the same "type" of rights guarantees, that is, extension of rights through negative prohibition. While conceding that the Fifteenth Amendment did "not establish the right of any citizen to vote," he admitted that it had been principally intended to benefit "colored persons" by conferring upon them the "right of suffrage." That being the case, Bradley was "inclined to the opinion" that the Enforcement Act of 1870 was valid since Congress had the power to secure that right "not only as against the unfriendly operation of state laws, but against outrage, violence, and combinations on the part of individuals, irrespective of state laws." Federal jurisdiction included any "war of race," whether of "civil strife or domestic violence," that resulted from the actions of groups, "private combinations," or "private outrage and intimidation."

At this point it would seem that Justice Bradley was not of a "contrary" opinion to Judge Woods. But then Bradley fell back on his earlier second distinction between state and federal authority.

Congress can protect black people from crimes of intimidation and violence, but *not* when such crimes "spring from . . . ordinary felonious intent." Those types of crimes are the "sole jurisdiction" of the states. Did the crimes Cruikshank and the others commit fall under this category? They did, because according to the justice, the counts of the indictment did not specifically allege that the violations of the law, including Tillman's murder, were committed "on account of their race, color, or previous condition of servitude." Bradley agreed with the defendants' attorneys' claim that the charges were drawn up in such a way as to be "vague and general." Since the language of the counts in the indictment failed to describe "a criminal offence known to any valid and constitutional law of the United States," the convictions based on those counts were invalid. Tillman and the other victims at Colfax Courthouse were most certainly African Americans, and Tillman (and many others) were most certainly murdered. But because of the defective indictment, Bradley concluded, the defendants had been tried in the wrong court!

Justice Bradley's views and intentions in his circuit court opinion on Cruikshank provoked speculation at the time and ever since. Why did he consider the Fourteenth and Fifteenth Amendments the same, and then interpret their meaning differently? If he was following the Supreme Court's narrowing of the Fourteenth Amendment's protection, why did he not do the same for the Fifteenth? Whatever his intentions, Louisiana Democrats expressed pleasure over the opinion. They felt it would not only put an end to the Grant Parish prosecutions, but stop all federal interference in state elections. Democrats also seemed to believe that Bradley reflected the intent of the entire Supreme Court to put an end to the federal government's enforcement efforts. District Attorney Beckwith's reaction was the opposite. He was clearly angered over the opinion, and accused Bradley of not having even read the indictments. Recalling that Bradley's appearance at the trial at been only at the very beginning of the second trial, and then after the verdicts had been handed down, Beckwith fumed that the justice's involvement had been a "nightmare" for the district attorney. Beckwith was especially upset at Bradley's reasoning, accusing the justice of exhibiting " a determination to demolish the law where . . . he [felt] equal to the task, and to demolish the indictment where he [could not] wrestle successfully with the law."

The district attorney probably had no cause to impute carelessness or incompetence on Bradley's part as far as understanding the indictment and the case. It was true, however, that the justice had drafted the opinion in the midst of a grueling round of travel, in the heat of summer, between Louisiana, Texas, and Washington, D.C. What seems most likely is Bradley saw this case as a way to bring both the issue of the constitutionality of the Enforcement Act and the meaning and scope of the Fifteenth Amendment before the Supreme Court. In this he clearly reflected Democratic sentiment that looked to ending all federal enforcement and political involvement. At the same time, he could not be unaware of either those Republicans who had their doubts about the federal government's role in protecting the rights of freedpeople in the South or those Republicans who believed that only a Supreme Court ruling could keep that role alive and effective.

Under federal court procedures at the time, the way to get the case before the Supreme Court was for Bradley to disagree with his colleague Woods, who had affirmed the convictions. Their rulings had been in response to the defendants' motion to "arrest" the judgment of the trial court. Bradley's and Woods's rulings in effect granted that motion, the immediate practical consequence of which was that the three defendants were immediately "discharged from custody." District Attorney Beckwith thereupon filed a "motion in error," in effect arguing that the circuit court wrongly affirmed the original motion and that because of the "division of opinion" of the judges on the motion, the case would be heard by the Supreme Court. This seems to have accorded with Bradley's intentions all along. Judicially, the same result would have happened if Bradley had merely expressed his "contrary" opinion, without explaining that opinion. By expressing his views, at some length, the justice was not only bringing the case before his brethren on the High Court, he was at the same time "clarifying" the issues that they would eventually address. Over the summer Bradley had sent copies of his opinion in the case to a number of friends, including Republican senator Frederick T. Frelinghuysen of New Jersey, who was a strong proponent of the Fifteenth Amendment and the Enforcement Acts. That fall, responding to comments made by the senator on his opinion, Justice Bradley admitted that "I am very glad that the Louisiana case is now in a position in which it can be brought before the Supreme Court and receive the deliberate and well-considered judgement of the whole Court."

CHAPTER 4

Lexington, Kentucky

Unlike Louisiana, the state of Kentucky remained in the Union during the Civil War, but like Maryland and the other border states, Kentucky was a slave state with a significant pro-Confederate population. Indeed, the Bluegrass State became infamous during the war as the "dark and bloody ground," where its citizens fought for both sides and against each other with a particular ferocity that did not stop with the war's end. The state's slave population, estimated at over 225,000 as of 1860, remained in bondage longer and slavery died more slowly than in the former Confederate states. Since the state was part of the Union it was not required by the federal government during Reconstruction to amend its prewar constitution, which protected slavery, and attempts to do so locally were defeated. The state even refused to ratify the Thirteenth Amendment. It took the introduction of the Freedman's Bureau and its programs, passage of the Civil Rights Act of 1866, and the Fourteenth Amendment for the message to get through to Kentuckians that slavery was indeed over. But the prejudice, fear, and hostility remained, and provoked the same outrage among parts of the white population as further south. Indeed, the extent and brutality of the violence and intimidation directed against blacks in Kentucky after 1866 often equaled that found anywhere in the states of former Confederacy.

Given these circumstances, the question of what civil and political rights freedpeople could expect to enjoy became central to Kentucky state politics once the war was over. While support for such rights would in large measure distinguish Republicans from Democrats, it was also true that among Republicans themselves, support for civil and political equality was often lukewarm at best. Before and during the Civil War most Republicans had seen themselves as essentially supporters of the Union and opponents of secession. Yet during the war they became increasingly suspicious of the national government, especially when the state was placed under martial law. Such suspicion of federal authority increased even more once the war ended and congressional Reconstruction began. There was widespread "aversion" to the growing federal presence in the state, particularly the Freedman's Bureau. As a result Kentucky Republicans had to constantly reconcile their party's principles, especially on race, with both their own political self-interest and their fear of yet more interference by Washington in the affairs of their beloved state.

This ambivalence was clearly obvious when it came to black voting rights and political participation. Under a state law passed back in 1799 both slaves and free blacks in Kentucky were specifically excluded from the ballot. Congressional Republicans' attempts to use the Fourteenth Amendment to force states to enfranchise blacks upon pain of loss of representation in Congress backfired in Kentucky, when one of their U.S. senators, Thomas C. McCreery, managed to slip through legislation relieving the state's political leaders from any disabilities under the amendment. Opposition to what Democrats referred to as the "nigger vote" and the desire to preserve the "White man's government" became the critical unifying theme for what had been disparate elements of the Democratic Party. But Republican support for voting rights was as much a matter of counting the additional votes they could expect to receive from a grateful African-American electorate as it was a widespread acceptance of notions of political equality. Indeed, ratification of the Fifteenth Amendment in March 1870 occurred without the Bluegrass State's approval, and even some Republicans complained that the amendment was an "unconstitutional" violation of the state's sovereignty. Republicans also acknowledged that the enfranchisement of nearly 100,000 potential supporters would definitely enhance their party's future.

For their part, African Americans in Kentucky greeted ratification of the Fifteenth Amendment as a historic event equal to, if not greater than, emancipation. Rallies and celebrations were held throughout the state, and the amendment was declared to be "the greatest event" in the nation's history. A month prior to ratification, the Republican Party sponsored the "First Republican Convention of the Colored Citizens of the State of Kentucky" in the state's capital, Frankfort. Perhaps prophetically, the meeting's site had to be changed because the public facility originally chosen would not admit blacks. The meeting in effect created a Black Republican Party that promised to work for the regular party as long as the latter promoted a "liberal spirit and enlightened legislation." From the outset, however, white Republicans showed little inclination to honestly integrate the two groups. Aside from some token appointments of prominent black leaders to party posts, few black candidates were slated to run for office on the party's ticket, and few were recipients of the kind of patronage positions and rewards used to cement real party unity. As one black Republican succinctly put it, "Our vote is all they want."

Such neglect paled in comparison to Democratic opposition. Ratification of the Fifteenth Amendment made Democrats in the state both fearful and outraged. On one hand they publicly warned blacks to stay out of politics; on the other they proclaimed that black votes would make no difference one way or another to the Democratic Party's future. As in other states, Democrats issued dire warnings of race war if blacks were allowed to vote, and spoke of enfranchisement as yet another unwanted and "unconstitutional" usurpation of state sovereignty by the federal government. In August 1870 elections were held for state and local offices, the first since ratification of the Fifteenth Amendment. The election was marked by riots and instances of violence, culminating in the lynching of two freedmen on election eve in the state capital. Democrats carried almost all the contests, but the margin of victory was slim, further emphasizing the potential significance of black voters. While the closeness of the contest reinforced Republican motivation to protect franchise rights, it also led to the formation of more Klan-type groups around the state. In some parts of the state a "reign of terror" was said to exist.

Even those Republicans protective of state sovereignty could not ignore what was happening, and some, like former slaveholder and unsuccessful gubernatorial candidate John Marshall Harlan, called for increased federal involvement in the state. Harlan even suggested the convening of what would amount to a permanent federal grand jury to investigate and punish Klan activity. Nor was Harlan alone. The federal government had officials in Kentucky who were willing and able to enforce federal civil and political rights protections. In 1866 Benjamin H. Bristow was appointed U.S. district attorney for the state. Bristow, like his friend Harlan, had become one of the leaders of the Republican Party. These Republicans attempted to project a more progressive image for the party and to embody the "liberalism" sought by Frankfort's black Republicans. Indeed, Bristow saw himself as a "champion" of the freedpeople and made a determined and successful effort to enforce the Civil Rights Act of 1866. In 1870, however, Bristow left for Washington following his appointment by President Grant as the first solicitor general. His assistant attorney and successor, Gabriel C. Wharton, continued Bristow's campaign to use federal authority to protect the rights of black citizens. Perhaps encouraged by the new solicitor general, both President Grant and Attorney General Akerman visited the state in the fall of 1871. They were especially interested in the extent of Klan activity in light of massive denials, including an official one by a state legislative investigating committee, that the Klan even existed in Kentucky. Armed now with the various Enforcement measures, Akerman returned to Washington and directed Wharton to use whatever means necessary to break up the Klan.

As it turned out, actual enforcement proved easier to order than carry out. As in the rest of the South, federal enforcement efforts were resisted by the targets and frustrated from within by the government itself. Witnesses and government officials were subject to constant harassment, intimidation, and worse. Defendants were protected by any means possible. In one notorious instance a white man accused of murdering a freedman was set free from a Frankfort jail by a group of Klansmen. The prosecution of those responsible for the breakout was complicated by the fact that one of the alleged participants belonged to a prominent Kentucky family. Ironically, the case was eventually dropped when the Kentucky legislature passed a law allowing African Americans to testify in court in criminal cases. According to District Attorney Wharton, the law would have enabled intimidated black witnesses to lie on behalf of the defendants.

At the same time, enforcement efforts in Kentucky were often sabotaged by the government itself. Justice Department promises of support, additional manpower, and sufficient funds to local officials never materialized, or when they did, were too little and too late. Attorney General Williams constantly urged his district attorneys and marshals to use "whatever means necessary" to enforce the election laws, but he could be equally consistent in his denials of requests from these same officials for the "means" to do so. At one point in the Frankfort case just described, District Attorney Wharton resorted to using his own private funds to continue the prosecution.

While federal officials in Kentucky struggled with the Klan and their use of violence and intimidation to nullify the Fifteenth Amendment, another more insidious form of resistance took shape, one that used the law itself and that reflected Kentucky's unique recent past as a border state. In those southern states that had been part of the Confederacy, like Louisiana, the fight to protect black voting rights was played out in the context of the struggle by Democrats to wrest political control from the hands of Republican regimes placed in power as a result of congressional Reconstruction after 1867. Since Kentucky did not go through the same process, Democrats never really lost control of the political and constitutional machinery of state government. They were therefore in a position to experiment with a variety of state and local laws to achieve what the Klan was doing outright in violation of the law. Ironically, what would come to be called the "Mississippi Plan" in the 1890s, involving state laws requiring literacy tests, grandfather-clause restrictions, and poll taxes to disfranchise black voters, was more like variations on a theme first set out by states like Kentucky during Reconstruction.

One common approach used was to modify city charters to exclude sections of the community with high concentrations of potential black voters. This form of gerrymandering was especially effective in Kentucky since once slavery ended, thousands of freedpeople left the farms and plantations of their bondage and flocked to the cities, where, not surprisingly, they congregated in the same areas. Indeed, by 1872 both the Louisville and Lexington metropolitan areas probably had African-American majorities as a result of this migration. Given this situation, the imposition of relatively lengthy residency requirements (three years in some places) also appeared as an effective tactic to limit, if not eradicate, the African-American vote. One locality even revived property ownership as a precondition for voting. What made this effort remarkable was that it was intended to increase the Democratic vote in the city more than to prevent blacks from voting. A small piece of land was purchased within the city by a group of ninety-three Democrats, who then divided their holding into "ribbon lots four inches wide," thereby entitling all ninety-three "owners" to vote even though none actually lived in town. Another tactic to discourage African-American voters was the use of the voice ballot, requiring voters in the state to publically announce their choices for office. (In 1871 the federal government would mandate the use of the secret, or Australian, ballot, and Kentucky would follow suit a year later.) Even more bizarre methods were considered in order to circumvent the Fifteenth Amendment's restriction on denial of voting rights based on race. Reportedly, the state legislature at one point considered a statute denying the franchise to anyone "who has wool or kinky hair on his scalp." This obviously referred to the presumed physical characteristic unique to African Americans.

In March of 1870 the Kentucky legislature passed an act to amend the city charter of Lexington, the second most populous city in the state. The act involved the structure of the city government and expanded the number of officials to be elected. Section 4 of the new law stated that to be entitled to vote at any city election a person "must be a free male citizen of the United States and the state of Kentucky and twenty one years of age." In addition, the act required residence in the city for at least six months prior to the election and sixty days' residence in the "area of the ward in which he resides." Most significant, each potential voter was required to have a "capitation tax" assessed them by the city on or before the January 15 preceding any election. In 1872 the city of Lexington fixed the capitation tax at $1.50. On January 30, 1873, citywide elections were held in Lexington. Although blacks outnumbered whites, the Democrats won by over a five-hundred-vote margin. According to one newspaper account the result was due to the capitation tax, which had "disfranchised about two-thirds of the Negro vote and left the Democrats an easy victory."

On February 17, 1873, a federal grand jury empaneled in the circuit court in Louisville brought indictments against three Lexington municipal election inspectors: Mathew Fouchee, Hiram Reese, and William Farnaugh. The actual indictment of the three men was a printed form some five pages in length, with blank spaces on which the grand jury and District Attorney Wharton merely had to fill in the specific information. It is therefore likely that other officials were similarly charged either at the time or later. In March 1877, almost two years after the Supreme Court's ruling in *Reese*, the defendants' attorney, B. F. Buckner, asked the clerk of the Supreme Court for an "official" copy of the Court's ruling. Buckner explained that he needed the copy so that he could ask the Court to dismiss the "forty odd other cases" which "by agreement were to abide by" the Court's ruling in *Reese*.

The indictment consisted of four counts, and in light of the Supreme Court's later ruling, it is important to consider them in some detail. Count one alleged that the three men charged were municipal inspectors at the January 30 election in Lexington, "charged by law with the duty of receiving, counting, certifying, registering, reporting, and giving effect to the vote in the election." It further alleged that at this election one William Garner, "a free male citizen of the United States of America and the State of Kentucky, of African descent" attempted to vote. It noted that Garner had resided in the state for more than two years, in the city of Lexington for more than a year, and in the ward where he attempted to vote for more than sixty days. It further stated that inspector Farnaugh had consented to receive his vote, but that Reese and Fouchee, "constituting the majority of said inspectors" had refused Garner's vote by demanding evidence of his having paid the capitation tax. The second count essentially repeated the information and charges of the first count with the addition of the following: that the defendants (Reese and Fouchee) did "unlawfully agree and concur with each other," that they would not receive the vote of any voter of African descent unless he should produce evidence, and that therefore the two had acted "with intent thereby to hinder, prevent, and obstruct, on account of their race and color, all voters of African descent."

The third count was the most unusual since it included an individual not specifically charged with any crime. According to the indictment James F. Robinson Jr. was the "lawful Collector" for the city of Lexington, charged with collecting and receiving "all taxes" payable to the city. On January 15, 1873, it was alleged that William Garner "in order that he might become qualified to vote" offered to pay the capitation tax to Robinson at his office, but that Robinson "then and there wrongfully refused on account of his (Garner's) race and color" to give Garner the opportunity to pay the tax. It also stated that Robinson had "then and there furnished and given to citizens of the white race" an opportunity to pay the tax. The fourth count repeated the same charge as the third, but tied everything together by alleging that at the time of his attempt to vote, William Garner had "presented" to the inspectors "his affidavit stating the offer to . . . Robinson . . . to pay the tax." Thus, Reese's and Fouchee's refusal to accept Garner's vote, the indictment charged, was "on account of the race and color of said William Garner contrary to the form of statute in such cases made and provided, and against the peace and dignity of the United States."

Exactly what "the form of statute in such cases" was did not appear anywhere in the indictment. Indeed, there was no mention of the Enforcement Act or the specific provisions of the act upon which the charges were supposedly based. That would not come out until the following November, by which time the defendants had secured the services of two "able counsel": Henry Stanbery, who had been busy defending those accused in the South Carolina Klan trials, and B. F. Buckner. On November 4, 1873, they filed a demurrer to the indictments in federal circuit court in Lexington. Although the timing of its presentation was different, this motion was similar to the motion "in arrest of judgement" made by Cruikshank's attorneys before Judge Woods and Justice Bradley in Louisiana. It essentially asked the court to reconsider the jury's verdict. The judges hearing the case in Kentucky were Circuit Court Judge Halmer H. Emmons and District Judge Bland Ballard. District Attorney Wharton argued on behalf of the government, and managed to convince the attorney general to authorize funds for hiring John M. Harlan to assist him.

The defendants' motion covered many of the same arguments that Cruikshank's attorneys had put forth in Louisiana. Stanbery and Buckner argued that all four counts of the indictment were "insufficient" in stating a defensible case in law and should therefore be thrown out. They also challenged the constitutionality of the same statute at issue in *Cruikshank*, the May 1870 Enforcement Act. The primary difference in this case, however, was the sections of that act questioned. Whereas in *Cruikshank* the indictments had been based on section 6, in *Reese* the relevant sections were 2, 3, and 4. Section 2 made it an offense for any person to interfere with or prevent any citizen from doing any act that "is or shall be required to be done as a prerequisite or qualification for voting." All citizens were to be given "the same and equal opportunity to perform such prerequisites [to vote], and to become qualified to vote without distinction of race, color, or previous condition of servitude." Section 3 specifically related to possible wrongful actions of public officials with respect to the exercise of franchise rights. It made it an offense for any individual "under the authority of the constitution or laws of any state" to "wrongfully" refuse to "receive, count, certify, register, report or give effect" to the vote of any citizen otherwise entitled to vote. Section 4 prohibited the use of "force, bribery, threats, intimidation, or other unlawful means" to "hinder, delay, prevent, or obstruct" any citizen from exercising their "right of suffrage." It also made it a crime for persons to "combine and confederate with others" in order to hinder or prevent citizens from voting.

In addition to the difference in sections of the Enforcement Act at issue in the two cases, there was also an important, if technical, difference in the claims made by defendants' attorneys at the Kentucky and Louisiana circuit court hearings. Cruikshank's lawyers had sought to show that the indictments were flawed because neither the indictment nor section 6 of the statute mentioned race as an element of the crimes charged (except for identifying the race of the two victims). They reasoned that if the statute was bad, any indictment based on it must also be bad. In the Kentucky hearing Stanbery and Buckner argued that the offenses set forth in sections 3 and 4 of the Enforcement Act did not "require" that the race, color, or previous condition of servitude of the victim be specified as the cause of any wrongful action that hindered or prevented the exercise of franchise rights. According to the attorneys, sections 3 and 4 only spoke of "without distinction of race." Therefore, Buckner and Stanbery argued, the indictments were flawed because they *did* allege that Reese's refusal to accept William Garner's vote was on account of Garner's race. Because race was so alleged in the indictment, Reese and the other two defendants were wrongfully put in the position of having to defend themselves against what amounted to an entirely new crime, one for which they had no prior notice! As confusing as these legal gymnastics appear, the exact wording of the indictments and the relevant sections of the Enforcement Act would become an important element in the Supreme Court's decision in both cases.

A month after the circuit court arguments in Kentucky, Judge Ballard sustained the demurrers to the indictment, without any explanatory opinion. However, since the other sitting judge in the case, Circuit Court Judge Edmunds, had evidently not agreed to the motion, District Attorney Wharton asked the court for a "certificate of division" that would enable him to appeal the ruling to the Supreme Court. This motion was granted, and the clerk of the court forwarded the materials to Attorney General

Williams in Washington. Wharton expressed his appreciation to the attorney general for the support he received from Washington and the "elaborate and able" arguments provided by John M. Harlan. The three defendants in the case, Reese, Fouchee, and Farnaugh, had been discharged from custody upon Judge Ballard's ruling on the demurrer. They were, however, required to post a five-hundred-dollar bond each to ensure their appearance should their convictions be upheld by the Supreme Court.

Thus, by the early part of 1874 there were two cases making their way toward a review by the United States Supreme Court that involved the constitutionality of the Enforcement Acts and the meaning and scope of the Fifteenth Amendment. The cases came from two different states and almost opposite factual circumstances. One case resulted from acts of horrific violence involving hundreds of persons, the other from the simple refusal of several election officials to accept the vote of one black man. Both represented a test of the future of the Republican Party's and the federal government's commitment to protect voting rights for African Americans in the South. Unlike his counterpart in Louisiana, District Attorney Wharton was neither upset at having his prosecution reviewed nor pessimistic about the outcome and impact of a Supreme Court ruling. Indeed, Wharton echoed Justice Bradley's sentiments in the *Cruikshank* case by hoping "that an early decision of the Supreme Court can be had on the validity and proper construction of the statute." What the district attorney and Justice Bradley, who after all was on the Court, could not know was that it would be another two years before they would get their decisions.

CHAPTER 5

The Supreme Court Hears the Cases

On February 3, 1874, the case of *United States v. Hiram Reese et al.* was docketed for hearing by the U.S. Supreme Court. Eight months later, on October 14, 1874, the case *United States v. William Cruikshank et al.* was similarly placed on the Court's agenda. At this time the Court did not yet meet in the magnificent marble structure across from the Capitol Building grounds that it presently occupies. Indeed, up until the Civil War the Supreme Court of the United States heard its cases in the basement of the Capitol. In 1860, following completion of new wings for the Senate and House chambers, the Court moved upstairs to what had formerly been the Senate chamber. The justices themselves were certainly satisfied, for their new quarters were more like a real court, with a raised bench, marble pillars, and adequate space for Court personnel.

While the location differed, the procedures and day-to-day functioning of the Supreme Court was much the same as today, and indeed was based on traditions going back to the early years of the Court's existence. By law the Supreme Court began its yearly session on "the first Monday in October," continuing with various breaks through the following spring. The Court usually heard oral arguments in cases during the week, and then held their deliberations on Saturday. Then, as now, each public session began with the same ceremony. The justices, robed, would enter the chamber as the Court's marshal admonished all to rise and then intoned the statement beginning with "Oyez, oyez, oyez" and ending with "God save the United States and this honorable Court." The justices sat in the same order as today, with the chief justice in the middle, the associate justice highest in seniority to his right, the next highest to his immediate left, and so on.

Two important differences in the Court's operation between the 1870s and the present are, however, worth noting. Attorneys who appear before the Court today to present oral arguments are under strict time constraints. During the nineteenth century they could be, and often were, more expansive in their presentations. And up until the end of the nineteenth century Supreme Court justices were also required to travel around the country "riding the circuit," sitting at least once a year as part of the circuit court panel. This duty was especially burdensome for justices whose circuits were in the South and West. Justice Stephen Field, whose West Coast circuit included his native California, had to make the trip by sail around South America, a ten-thousand-mile trip that could take weeks. Even after the completion of the transcontinental railroad in 1869, circuit duty was the acknowledged "great albatross" of Supreme Court duty.

The Court in 1874 consisted of nine justices, eight associate justices and one chief justice. That number itself had varied over the years, from a low of six in 1789 to a high of ten in 1863, and then back to nine by 1870. The Court's chief justice, Morrison R. Waite, was also the most recent appointee to the bench. He took his seat on the tribunal in January 1874, less than a month prior to the filing of *Reese*. The circumstances behind Waite's appointment were hardly auspicious. Following the death of Chief Justice Salmon P. Chase on May 7, 1873, President Grant unsuccessfully attempted to appoint at least three other persons, including Attorney General George Williams, before an "exhausted" Senate finally confirmed Waite. An Ohio attorney, Waite had served on the Toledo city council and in the Ohio state legislature. At the time of his appointment he was in Switzerland serving on a diplomatic mission for the U.S. government, negotiating claims against the British government stemming from the Civil War. What Waite lacked in experience and legal intellect, he made up for with strength of character and the managerial skills necessary to hold together a group of diverse and potentially divisive justices. Even those who disagreed with the Court's opinions conceded that as chief justice, Waite helped restore a good deal of the Supreme Court's prestige lost by its "self-inflicted wound," the 1857 decision in the *Dred Scott* case.

The senior member of the Court, and the lone Democratic appointee from the pre–Civil War years, was Nathan Clifford. Clifford was a New Englander appointed by President James Buchanan in 1858. His age and increasing senility by the early 1870s proved an ongoing challenge to his colleagues and to the chief justice's patience and good humor, and would be a factor in the Court's delay in announcing its opinion in *Reese* and *Cruikshank*. Justice David Davis's appointment in 1862 had largely been the result of his personal friendship with and campaign service to President Lincoln. Davis made no secret of either his dissatisfaction with life on the Supreme Court, which he compared to "hard labor," or his political aspirations. In 1872 he unsuccessfully sought the Liberal Republican nomination for president, and in 1877 he resigned his seat on the Court following his election as senator from Illinois. Another Lincoln appointee, Californian Stephen J. Field, proved to be an outspoken and forceful figure during what became one of the longest tenures of any Supreme Court justice in history. As chief justice of the California Supreme Court at the time of his elevation in 1863, Field had already begun to display his unique, if not dogmatic, concern for the protection of private, meaning business, property rights against governmental interference.

While Field and Davis provided the personalities on the Court, Justices Joseph Bradley and Samuel Miller were by common consensus its dominant intellectual forces. Miller was an Iowa attorney with no public experience when President Lincoln nominated him in 1862; his analytic skills, strong nationalism, and prodigious output of over six hundred opinions over a twenty-eight-year career on the High Court had a significant impact on constitutional development in the late nineteenth century. He also seemed to have a rather profound regard for his own abilities, while he could be equally dismissive of those of his brethren. Miller resented Waite, believing that he himself should have been Chase's replacement as chief justice, and he engaged in a lengthy feud with Justice Noah Swayne. In the area of civil rights Miller would perhaps achieve his greatest notoriety when he wrote the majority opinion in the *Slaughterhouse Cases* in 1873, in which the Court fatally narrowed the scope of the Fourteenth Amendment's civil rights protections. Yet eleven years later Miller upheld strong federal authority over the electoral process in his opinion in the *Yarbrough* case.

Like Miller, Joseph P. Bradley had no significant public career prior to his nomination in 1870. A prominent Newark, New Jersey, attorney whose main clients were businessmen, Bradley was a Republican who supported the Union and opposed slavery, but was probably closer to most white southerners in his views on racial equality. His impact on the Court, however, would turn less on his legal acumen than on his close friendship with the chief justice. Indeed, Chief Justice Waite openly admitted his respect for Bradley's advice and his reliance on Bradley for helping shape his own opinions. Waite once wrote to Bradley about an opinion the chief justice was working on: "I will take the credit, and you shall do the work, as usual." As previously described, it was Bradley's circuit court opinion in *Cruikshank* that brought the case before the Supreme Court.

The three remaining justices on the Court in 1875 were Noah H. Swayne, William Strong, and Ward Hunt. Swayne, an Ohio attorney, has been characterized as "Lincoln's first and worst appointment." Appointed to replace fellow Ohioan John McLean, Swayne had a nineteen-year career on the Court that yielded few significant opinions, but he was consistent in following his Republican beliefs in support of national authority and civil rights. His most noteworthy achievement in this regard was his dissenting opinion in the *Slaughterhouse Cases*, in which he forcefully defended the purpose of the Fourteenth Amendment as a protection not only for the privileges and immunities of African Americans, but for all citizens. Swayne's final years of the bench were marked by a noticeably diminished mental capacity. Despite the efforts of his colleagues to convince him to resign, he did not do so until President Hayes agreed to replace him with yet another Ohioan, Stanley Matthews. Justice William Strong, a devoutly religious railroad attorney from Pennsylvania and a judge on that state's supreme court, was appointed by Grant to the Supreme Court at the same time as Bradley. Like many Republicans by this time, Strong cared more about economic issues than civil rights and the problems of the South, and during his ten-year career on the Court almost always sided with the increasing number of justices, especially Field, hostile to state economic regulation. The ninth justice was Ward Hunt, a New York Republican. Hunt had been chief judge of that state's highest court, the court of appeals, at the time of his appointment by President Grant in 1882. But Hunt's appointment was due less to his legal or judicial reputation than the support of the powerful senator from New York, Roscoe Conkling. Hunt's tenure on the Court lasted only nine years, and perhaps his one shining moment would come with his dissent in *Reese*. During the 1878 term of the Court Hunt suffered a debilitating stroke, but refused to resign for another three years until Congress approved his pension.

Once the cases were placed on the Court's docket, attorneys for both sides formally indicated their involvement in the case, submitted their written briefs, and set a date for oral arguments. In both cases Attorney General George H. Williams and Solicitor General Samuel Field Phillips represented the government's side, and from the outset it was clear that they had their work cut out for them. Williams, as discussed above, had been a controversial appointment from the beginning. Evidence that he had replaced an Oregon federal attorney about to bring charges under the Enforcement Acts against a Williams political ally did not bode well for his commitment to making a strong case for the acts' constitutionality. Phillips, a North Carolina attorney when appointed by Grant to replace Bristow as solicitor general, was another matter. Like other southerners Phillips had gone "from white supremacist to egalitarian" in the years following the Civil War. His dedication and competence was reflected in the fact that he served as the number-two person in the Justice Department until 1885, one of the longest tenures of any solicitor general. Phillips consistently, if not always successfully, supported strong federal authority over political and civil rights enforcement. His briefs and arguments before the Supreme Court defending such authority reflected his personal feelings that the future of African Americans in the South depended on the simple principle that they be treated "like all other men."

To say that the defendants in both cases were well represented would be an understatement. The attorneys who had argued the cases in the Kentucky Circuit Court, Henry Stanbery and B. F. Buckner, appeared in the Supreme Court on behalf of Reese and Fouchee. Buckner, a Louisville attorney and former judge, came from one of the most prominent Kentucky families. Stanbery, as noted earlier, had been an attorney general himself and had been involved recently in defending the South Carolina Klansmen prosecuted under the Enforcement Acts. The defense "team" of eight attorneys for Cruikshank was even more impressive. It included Maryland senator, and former attorney general, Reverdy Johnson, who had worked with Stanbery on the South Carolina cases. Assisting Johnson were former Supreme Court justice John A. Campbell and Congressmen Phillip Phillips and David Dudley Field, brother of Supreme Court Justice Stephen J. Field. The rest of the defense team included Ezekiel J. Ellis, David S. Bryon, William R. Witaker, and Robert H. Marr, the Louisiana attorney who had represented the defendants from the moment of their indictment.

The brief submitted in *Reese* by Stanbery and Buckner covered the same points and made the same arguments they had presented before the circuit court. They began with a general attack on the Enforcement Acts themselves. The Fifteenth Amendment prohibited interference with the right to vote "by any state on account of race." The only way in which a state could interfere with that right was if the "legislative branch" passed a law. That law might then be challenged first in the state courts, and if upheld, appealed to the federal Supreme Court. If this were so, the attorneys argued, then the sections of the Enforcement Acts under review in this case were unconstitutional. The sections were unconstitutional because they referred specifically to the possible wrongful actions of individual citizens, or groups of citizens, and not any state laws. This suggestion of what would come to be called the "state action" doctrine was based on a extremely narrow distinction between state legislation and those individuals, in this case election "inspectors," who presumably were acting on behalf of and as representatives of the state.

Stanbery and Buckner's brief then focused on sections 3 and 4 of the Enforcement Act of May 1870. They argued that section 3 was invalid for several related reasons. For one thing, the attorneys claimed, the statute was overly broad and vague as to the exact nature of the crime subject to punishment. What evidence could be presented to prove that an election official "wrongfully prevented" a person from voting on account of that person's race? The brief noted that "(t)he only evidence which the election officers shall hear . . . is the affidavit of the voter that he was wrongfully prevented from registering. . . . He may be totally disqualified as to age, residence, &c., yet under this remarkable statute, if he makes oath that he was wrongfully prevented from registering, the judges must receive his vote."

In addition, defense counsel argued that section 3 was invalid because it did not explicitly require that any wrongful hindrance or prevention "be on account of race." Indeed, there was no limitation on what could cause the wrongful act. The practical implication of this was that the language of the statute was too broad. An election official's refusal "may result from private malice, partizan [*sic*] malignity, or even an honest mistake of the law." Therefore, "every possible motive . . . is embraced by the act," and the act itself was an inappropriate means to prevent discrimination based on race. Section 4 had the same weaknesses. Without the words "on account of race," any use of bribery, force, threats, or "unlawful" means to prevent a voter from voting becomes a crime, "no matter whether race or color had any connection with it or not." Since the Fifteenth Amendment only proscribed discrimination or wrongful acts based on race, the defense counsel concluded that the statutes were unconstitutional.

Given the significance of the case and the government's desire to have a positive constitutional ruling on the election statutes, it is surprising how "muddled" and ineffective the government's brief submitted in *Reese* was. This is all the more remarkable inasmuch as Attorney General Williams and Solicitor General Phillips had taken the unusual step in November 1874 of withdrawing their original brief to make changes in it. After reciting the various counts under which the defendants were convicted, the revised brief began with an unusual argument. The government's brief argued that the 1870 Enforcement Act was constitutional "under the Constitution as originally framed; or, at all events, after the adoption of the Fourteenth Amendment." Using citations from the framers of the Constitution and the Court's recent ruling in the *Slaughterhouse Cases*, the brief contended that among the constitutionally guaranteed "immunities and privileges" of all citizens is the "elective franchise." The attorney general, however, could cite no judicial ruling or legal citation after 1789 that supported the idea that voting rights were included in the Constitution "as originally framed." Morever, the brief's interpretation of the Supreme Court's ruling in *Slaughterhouse* was simply wrong. But then as quickly as it appeared, the entire argument was abandoned. For the attorney general and the solicitor general, the "real" issues raised in the present case "require a consideration of the XVth Amendment of the Constitution."

Williams and Phillips's analysis of the Fifteenth Amendment was as unusual as their opening argument. They went through a word-by-word exegesis of the amendment and a precise chronology behind its formation that focused almost entirely on its wording and not its intent. The authors seemed more interested in a display of their knowledge of Latin legal proverbs and maxims than in the relationship of the Fifteenth Amendment to the protection of black voting rights. However, in a circuitous way they did respond to several of the arguments in the defendants' brief. They rejected the proposition that Reese and the others had acted as private individuals. As election officials the three men were acting under the authority of the state, and "if by means of authority derived from the state [an agent] has power to act in the way in which he did, his act obtains its force from the state, irrespective of the extent to which the agent observed or violated the rules laid down for his direction." In other words, the defendants' actions in refusing Garner's vote were the actions of the State of Kentucky as proscribed in the Fifteenth Amendment's "No state shall . . ." provision.

The government's response to the defendants' challenge to the constitutionality of relevant sections of the Enforcement Act was even more remarkable. Williams and Phillips in effect conceded that the sections may have been "over-broad" because the statutes did not require the specific allegation of race as the reason for the wrongful actions. Indeed, they argued that the statutes had been intentionally drawn that way! "Although the particular race whose needs were the motive of the amendment were Africans," they wrote, "yet it protects *all races, &c.*, as appears from the generality of the language." Moreover, this was confirmed by the "fact" that Congress had rejected an amendment "proposing to confine its operation to Africans." In Williams's and Phillips's minds the Fifteenth Amendment protected "all citizens" from racial discrimination, and therefore sections 3 and 4 of the Enforcement Act should not be construed to protect one particular race, but all qualified voters "generally." In that case, the charges against the defendants were valid precisely because they were based on language "directed against unlawful hindrances of that sort upon any account and by any person." That the two sections had a "wider application" than was needed in the present case had one critical consequence. The fact that William Garner was a "person of color" had become irrelevant.

What either the justices or defense counsel thought of this "color-blind" interpretation of the Fifteenth Amendment and the Enforcement Acts is uncertain. No formal record exists of the oral arguments made by both sides in this case before the Supreme Court. What is known is that the Supreme Court's eventual ruling in *Reese* completely ignored these arguments, not even bothering to reject them. The attorney general and solicitor general's brief did not merely fall short in responding to the defendant's claims, it left out the obvious claims about the intent of the Fifteenth Amendment and the overall purpose of the Enforcement Acts. It virtually conceded to the defense the principle that among the rights the national government had the obligation, as well as the authority, to protect when it came to African

Americans was the right to vote. Why this brief was filed is equally uncertain, but clearly invites speculation. The best that could be said for the government's presentation was that the attorney general assumed that the justices were already familiar with broader constitutional arguments, and that the brief was intended to provided them alternative or additional support. Possibly, the attorney general also believed there was no better way to defend the district attorney's omission of race in the indictments.

The government's brief submitted by the attorney general and Solicitor General Williams in *U.S. v. Cruikshank* was hardly more effective. Aside from an opening summary of the original indictment counts, the relatively short document made absolutely no mention of African Americans or the Fifteenth Amendment, and made only passing reference to the Enforcement Acts! In fact the government began its argument by virtually ignoring all the issues raised in Justice Bradley's circuit court opinion, including the opportunity to focus the Court's attention on interpreting the Fifteenth Amendment. As in the *Reese* brief, the government seem to concede any argument premised on a strong national authority to protect citizens' rights. In light of Bradley's ambiguous interpretation of the Fifteenth Amendment and his refusal to directly strike down the Enforcement Acts, the government's presentation was clearly remarkable for what it didn't do and what it conceded to the other side from the outset.

Instead, Williams and Phillips "confined" themselves to discussing only two counts of the original indictment. The two counts (the fourteenth and sixteenth) were based on section 6 of the 1870 Enforcement Act and involved the charge of "conspiracy." Their entire brief was devoted to proving that conspiracy was a "crime cognizable by the United States." As in their *Reese* brief, the *Cruikshank* brief cited extended, and often confusing, quotations from the framers of the Constitution, English case law, and "text-books and digests," in order to "prove" that the crime of conspiracy was "cognizable" under federal authority. The attorney general and solicitor general attempted to show that the words "threaten, injure, oppress, and intimidate" in section 6 of the Enforcement Act were legally valid terms that constituted the "facts" of a charge for the crime for conspiracy, and not, as defendant's claimed, a "legal conclusion" to be proven. The issue was not just the crime of conspiracy, but whether the alleged conspiracy prevented or hindered a citizen in the "free exercise of any right or privilege granted or secured" by the Constitution. This led to the question of what rights were so protected. The attorney general and solicitor general briefly disposed of this issue by arguing that the right to vote in federal elections was beyond doubt a "Federal right" and that "nothing could be said to impeach the validity of Federal legislation" to protect that right. Perhaps aware of the irony, and intending to give "no offence," they compared this obvious national right to vote with the "well known" right to "reclaim fugitives from labor," that is, fugitive slaves, and quoted nearly the entire Supreme Court ruling in *Prigg v. Pennsylvania* from 1842. Because the victims of the conspiracy, Nelson and Tillman, were citizens of the United States and not "another political society," the conspiracy to "deprive" them of their right to vote "may well be" indictable in federal courts.

Compared to this anemic presentation, the four lengthy briefs submitted by the defendants' attorneys formed a full-scale assault on the constitutionality of the Enforcement Act and their clients' prosecution. Although each of the briefs highlighted different issues and arguments, a number of common themes emerged. All the briefs agreed that the sections of the Enforcement Act with which the defendants were charged were unconstitutional, based on the notion that "the powers of the federal government are delegated, and strictly limited." According to this idea the national government was prohibited from doing that which it was not given authority to do in the Constitution. But what about the protection of citizens' rights, for example, those found in the Bill of Rights, the first ten amendments to the Constitution? Indeed, the defendants were convicted of conspiracy to deny their victims at least two provisions of the Bill of Rights: the right to peacefully assemble and the right to bear arms.

According to the defendants' counsel, the purpose of the Bill of Rights was not to grant citizens any specific rights, but to protect citizens from their infringement by the federal government. These amendments "were the result of the apprehension of the people that the federal government would become too powerful, and might ultimately destroy the rights of the states and liberties of the people." All four briefs had it as settled constitutional doctrine, going back to Chief Justice John Marshall's 1835 decision in *Barron v. Baltimore*, that the Bill of Rights was not a limit on state authority, but only on the federal government. Those specific rights set forth in the amendments were not intended to "secure any of the rights in question against interference either by state governments or by individuals." With the exception of specific limitations on state authority, such as the ban on ex post facto laws, or laws impairing the obligation of contracts, "the entire domain of the privileges and immunities of citizens of the States . . . lay within the constitutional and legislative power of the States, and without that of the federal government."

This very limited view of federal authority should not have been surprising. It reflected the states' rights constitutionalism of the South in the years leading up to the Civil War. One of the attorneys, John A. Campbell, had made much the same argument as a Supreme Court justice in his concurring opinion in the *Dred Scott* case upholding slavery. Wisely, none of the attorneys, including Campbell, cited that case. But it did raise the crucial issue as to whether or not the three postwar amendments changed in any significant way the powers of the federal government to protect individual rights, either those existing rights found in the Bill of Rights or any new rights that may or may not have been created under the new amendments. All of the defendants' briefs agreed that the limits on federal authority with respect to the right of individuals to peacefully assemble or bear arms were as restrictive now as they had been in 1835. With respect to these rights "the authority of a state is complete, unqualified, and exclusive," and the people within each state "remain in full and entire possession of all the powers of self-government not surrendered or granted by the constitution." None of the provisions of the Bill of Rights had been nationalized or "incorporated" by any of the postwar amendments.

But those rights that were part of the new amendments were more problematic, especially since all three amendments did explicitly refer to "states." The Thirteenth Amendment abolished slavery everywhere in the United States. Once those states where slavery had been legal ratified the Thirteenth Amendment, that amendment had become fully "executed." Only if some state attempted to reinstitute slavery could Congress presumably then act. But what about the Fourteenth Amendment? According to this amendment, "no state shall make or enforce any law which shall abridge the privileges and immunities of citizens of the United States, nor shall any State deprive any person of life, liberty or property without due process of law, nor shall any state deny to any person within its jurisdiction the equal protection of the laws." The argument had been made, by both supporters and opponents of the Enforcement Acts, that the rights protected by the acts referred to the "privileges and immunities" clause of the Fourteenth Amendment. But what were the specific privileges and immunities subject to federal protection? Did it mean that Congress now had within its power "the entire domain of civil rights heretofore belonging exclusively to the states"? The defense argued that the Supreme Court had already resolved this issue in its *Slaughterhouse* decision two years earlier. In that case the Court had narrowly defined what constituted federally protected privileges and immunities under the Fourteenth Amendment. These included freedom of travel on the high seas and the right to go to the seat of government to petition grievances. When it came to protecting other civil rights, those of more immediate relevance to freedpersons in the South than ocean travel, the Fourteenth Amendment had produced no "revolution" in federal authority. Those civil rights previously "reserved" to the protection of the states remained completely "within" the states.

Defendants' briefs also raised the same set of objections as those presented by the defense in *Reese*, albeit in a more extreme form, with respect to the idea of state action. Section 6 of the Enforcement Act was unconstitutional because it referred to crimes committed by *individuals* and not the states. The Fourteenth and Fifteenth Amendments placed certain restrictions on the states, and "the only way in which these amendments can be violated, is by the legislative or conventional acts of a 'State'." As a result, the people of a state, acting in their "personal and individual capacity" may in fact do what a state is prohibited from doing, and the briefs were remarkably candid in what that meant for "the people." It meant "they may take a man's life, in open combat, or by a secret taking off, they may rob him of his property . . . , they may restrain him of his liberty, and by violence and intimidation prevent him from voting." All these things "have not violated these amendments, because these individuals are not the state, and their acts are not the acts of the 'State'." Did defense counsel mean to suggest that it was actually legal for people in, say, Louisiana, to kill or rob, or intimidate others? Not really, although some may have disagreed. This was merely the extreme logical extension of the defendants' claim that all ordinary crimes or criminal activity, including those set forth in the indictments based on the Enforcement Act, remained the complete and absolute responsibility of state governments. More importantly, the distinction between state and federal authority over such "ordinary" crimes was one Justice Bradley had relied on in his circuit court opinion.

However, Cruikshank and the other defendants were not charged with or convicted of Tillman's murder or the denial of Nelson's rights. They were charged and convicted under the section of the Enforcement Act that made it a crime to "conspire" to do so. The defense's objection was the same. The crime of conspiracy had never been, nor could it be, a federal crime. There was no constitutional or legal authority for it to be so, and like other "regular" crimes, it was "reserved" to the state governments to prohibit. The government's brief had gone back to English precedents and doctrine to argue that prohibiting the crime of conspiracy was a valid and necessary tool of any national government to protect itself, as well as the liberty of and order among its citizens. The defendants' briefs used the same cases and writings to prove the opposite. The defense demonstrated how in the past governments had used charges of conspiracy as an instrument of tyranny and "vengeance" through prosecutions carried out by "dependent and subservient judges" against those individuals or groups fighting for their rights and liberties.

Another issue raised by the defense briefs was the specific wording of the statute itself. Defendants' brief in *Reese* had focused on the vagueness of the statutes in defining a specific crime, but had used only the general proposition that this was "unfair." The briefs in *Cruikshank*, particularly the one submitted by Campbell, found a more specific objection. The conspiracy sections of the Enforcement Acts as drafted were violations of the Fifth Amendment to the Constitution, because they did not "inform" the accused of what specific rights or privileges he was accused of, or might be accused of, conspiring to prevent or hinder. To defend themselves against a possible charge under this statute, Campbell argued, would require that a person "know the constitutional and statutory law . . . by which rights, privileges and immunities have been granted and secured." That is, a person would have to be a constitutional scholar like Campbell.

The final target of the defense's briefs in Cruikshank was the Fifteenth Amendment. For the most part their argument really just extended and summarized many of their previous points. According to the defense, the Fifteenth Amendment was intended only to prevent either the state governments or the national government from denying or abridging the right to vote using race or color as a condition. This was the "only" restriction placed on the states. All other qualifications for voting, as well as the conduct of elections, remained "completely" within the purview of the states. The briefs agreed that the sections of the Enforcement Act being reviewed, and the indictments based on those sections, were "bad." They were bad because there was no requirement to prove that the defendants' actions "were on account of the victims' race or color." Nor, the defense asserted, was there any proof presented "in the record" of the case that the actions of the defendants had been on account of their victims' race.

Unfortunately, no complete record exists of the oral presentations made to the Court by either side in either of these cases. There is, however, one exception: a printed version, consisting of thirty-six pages, of the oral presentation made by attorney David

Dudley Field on behalf of Cruikshank and the other defendants. The major portion of Field's arguments centered on demonstrating that the Enforcement Acts, and indeed all federal civil rights legislation since the end of the Civil War, were unconstitutional. He conceded that the intent or "plan" of the three Reconstruction Amendments was to "give the blacks all the rights which the whites enjoyed." His concern centered on what Congress could or could not do to enforce the prohibitions contained in the amendments. The key for Field was the sections in each of these amendments authorizing Congress to pass "appropriate" enforcement legislation. Congress, he maintained, had misread the "natural interpretation" of what constituted appropriate legislation as "understood by the people." Historically and philosophically, governments could "enforce" a right only through a "judicial remedy." Therefore, Congress could extend or protect rights only by providing avenues for redress in the courts, not by creating new categories of crimes and violations punishable in the courts. Congress could enable citizens to challenge state laws that they claimed denied them the right to vote because of their race, but it could not create "new" laws for whose violation states, or their officials, or their citizens, might be punished.

Field's peroration was of course a variation on the federalism argument presented by several of the other defense attorneys. It was an argument for states' sovereignty without resort to the extreme, and still discredited, states' rights doctrines of the pre–Civil War years. He did not deny federal powers, he merely argued that Congress had crossed the line separating federal and state authority. It was a moderate, and powerful, argument, but it also came with a warning. If the Court approved this legislation they would be approving in effect a "new theory of Government" and an interpretation of federalism "that the people never contemplated." Indeed, he concluded, "If the validity of the present legislation is affirmed, one may affirm the validity of legislation upon any subject concerning life, liberty, property, and protection by the law."

It is tempting in hindsight to summarize the arguments made by both sides in these two cases by way of evaluating the quality of their writing and the persuasiveness of their arguments. An evaluation of these writings must be tempered by the possibility that during these years the written briefs submitted in Supreme Court cases played a less critical role than today in persuading the justices of the rightness of one side or the other. Briefs submitted today generally are far longer and more numerous than their predecessors, probably as a consequence of attorneys having such a short time to present their oral arguments today.

To say that overall the defendants' briefs were better or stronger may be valid but not necessarily surprising. They had to be, since they were not only challenging their clients' convictions, they were asking the Supreme Court to declare an act of Congress unconstitutional. The Supreme Court had used judicial review only twice since it had first acquired this power in *Marbury v. Madison* back in 1801, and both times the Court had damaged its prestige by doing so. The first time was the "self-inflicted wound" in their 1857 *Dred Scott* decision. Most recently the Supreme Court in 1870 had declared the Legal Tender Acts invalid, only to reverse themselves within a year amid charges that President Grant had "packed the Court" by appointing Justices Strong and Bradley, who were known to have favored the measures. In this context the defendants' briefs in both cases were comprehensive and tactically strong. They examined all the possible issues, from the wording and defects in the indictments to the broader constitutional questions. What seems certain, at least in the *Cruikshank* briefs, is that the defendants' counsel had carefully studied Justice Bradley's circuit court ruling and crafted their arguments to reflect his views. With the exception of states'-rightist John Campbell's contribution, the briefs all emphasized the dual-citizenship approach taken by the Court in the *Slaughterhouse Cases* with regard to the Fourteenth Amendment.

CHAPTER 6

The Supreme Court Decides

Given the expectations surrounding both cases, it was perhaps surprising that the Supreme Court did not announce its verdict in either *Reese* or *Cruikshank* until almost two years after the cases were first filed with the Court, and almost a year after the first oral arguments were heard. A little more than a week following the oral arguments in *Reese* on January 13 and 14, 1875, the Court decided to hold the case "under advisement," presumably to await the scheduled arguments in *Cruikshank* on March 1. Those arguments were not heard until the end of the month, by which time the Court's summer adjournment was at hand, so that *Cruikshank* was likewise held under advisement by the Court. Both cases were scheduled for the fall term, and according to the chief justice's own docket book, were "set for hearing Oct 30." In fact, the word "hearing" was deceptive, since it suggested another round of oral arguments that never happened. What the term did reflect was that the Court had decided to decide these cases together.

One of the more problematic aspects of historical reconstructions of Supreme Court decisions is that one of the key steps in the Court's decision-making process was, and remains, cloaked in secrecy. By long-standing tradition, no minutes or formal account of the weekly Court conferences are kept. Thus, how the justices actually reached their decision is often a matter of piecing together a puzzle in which some significant pieces are missing. The record in *Reese* and *Cruikshank* is an example, and the story of how the Court reached its decision in these two cases is largely based on Chief Justice Waite's docket book and materials by and about individual justices.

According to Waite's records the Supreme Court agreed on November 6 to affirm the lower court rulings overturning the convictions in both cases. In the *Cruikshank* case the vote was unanimous, with all the justices listed as voting to affirm. The outcome in *Reese* appeared more complicated. The vote was not unanimous, and there was disagreement over counts two and four of the indictment. The second count of the indictment, it may be recalled, charged the two election supervisors, Reese and Fouchee, with "unlawfully" agreeing and concurring with each other not to receive the vote of any voter of African-American descent. Count four had charged the two supervisors, along with the unindicted tax collector, James Robinson, with refusing to accept William Garner's vote "on account of his race." Justices Bradley, Field, Davis, Swayne, Strong, and Waite all voted to affirm the lower court's ruling and agreed that both counts two and four were "bad." Justice Miller voted to affirm, but was noted as finding both counts good *and* bad. Justice Clifford voted to reverse, but like the majority found both counts bad. Only Justice Hunt voted to uphold the convictions, agreeing that both counts of the indictment were "good."

Early on, the chief justice decided to write the opinions in both cases himself, admitting that "when I supposed the enforcement cases would be decided on constitutional grounds I felt it to be my duty to try and write the opinion myself." Once the Court had unanimously decided to focus on the indictments in *Reese* and *Cruikshank*, he instead assigned the opinion writing to Justice Clifford. In asking Clifford to draft the opinions, Waite noted, "You are perfectly familiar with criminal law and I am not." Clifford agreed "with pleasure" to draft the opinions, since "questions of criminal pleading are quite familiar to me." On November 20 Clifford's draft opinions were presented to the Court, but a week later the *Reese* opinion was "disapproved" by the justices, at which point Waite took over writing both opinions. The chief justice never stated his reasons for doing this. Most likely, Clifford's drafts, as evidenced in his concurring opinion in *Reese*, completely avoided the constitutional issues that Waite and the other justices felt needed to be addressed. The chief justice may have assumed that at least in *Cruikshank* these questions would be faced, especially given Justice Bradley's earlier circuit court ruling. In addition, in the *Reese* voting Justice Hunt had supported both the indictments and the statute, and Justice Miller had indicated his concern over the statute but not the indictments. In any case, Waite evidently now felt it was his responsibility to deal with the constitutional issues presented. He drafted the opinions, and on March 25, 1875, read them to his colleagues. They were approved, and two days later the decisions were announced to the public.

Chief Justice Waite's opinion in *U.S. v. Reese* was relatively short, covering just over six pages in the printed Court reports. He began by noting that the government had already conceded that the first and third counts of the indictment would not be defended, and that all claims "not arising" out of the enforcement of the Fifteenth Amendment should not be considered. Given this concession, Waite concluded, the Court need only decide a single issue. That issue was whether or not the relevant sections of the Enforcement Act of May 1871 under which the defendants were indicted "can be made effective." After restating the first four sections of the Enforcement Act in their entirety, Waite explained that the two counts of the indictments under review by the Court, counts two and four, were based only on sections 3 and 4 of the act, respectively. Section 3 had made it a crime for any official to prevent a person from either voting or performing the "pre-requisites" necessary in order to vote. Section 4 forbade any person to "combine and confederate with others" for the purpose of wrongfully preventing persons from voting by refusing to "receive, count, certify, register, report or give effect" to their vote. Thus, by this process of elimination the chief justice narrowed his analysis to determining whether or not only two sections of the May 1870 Enforcement Act were constitutional.

Waite admitted that Congress did have the authority to protect those "rights and immunities created by or dependent upon the Constitution." Moreover, the "form and manner" of such protection was likewise up to "legislative discretion," and "these may be varied to meet the necessities of the particular right to be protected." But there was the problem. In what would become the most quoted sentence from his opinion in *Reese*, Waite declared that the "Fifteenth Amendment does not confer the right of suffrage upon any one." The amendment did invest citizens with a "new constitutional right," but that right was not the right to vote. Rather, that right was "exemption from discrimination in the exercise of the elective franchise on account of race, color, or previous condition of servitude." Prior to the Fifteenth Amendment, states could and did exclude citizens from the elective franchise based on age, property, education, or race. Now they could not use race, and Congress could enforce this right by "appropriate legislation."

That brought the chief justice to the question of whether or not the two sections of the Enforcement Act were constitutional. Were the sections of the statute "appropriate legislation" as authorized by the second section of the Fifteenth Amendment? The issue, as both sides essentially agreed in their briefs, was the language of the sections and their interpretation. Waite acknowledged this dilemma. On one hand, it could be claimed that section 3 was overbroad because it forbade wrongful refusals to accept affidavits, or ballots, by an official without limiting such refusals specifically to those done on account of race. At the same time he recognized that if section 3 was "construed with those [sections of the Act] which precede it, and to which it is claimed, it refers," it might indeed then be interpreted as being limited to denials on account of race.

It came down to how one "construed" such language, and Waite started out by equivocating, admitting that there were two possible ways to go in this as well. This was a "penal statute" and as such had to be construed "strictly," but at the same time "not so strictly as to defeat the clear intention of Congress"! The words of the statute must also be "understood in the sense they were obviously used." For Waite the "strict" interpretation of the language became necessary for two reasons. First, because these statutes marked an "important" and "radical" change in the role of the federal government with regard to election laws and state authority. In that case, it was incumbent that such statutes be "explicit" in their terms. "Nothing should be left to construction if it can be avoided," for either those subject to the law or those charged with enforcing the law. The second justification for a strict interpretation of the language of the statute reflected Waite's view of the judiciary's role. According to the chief justice, it was not the duty of the courts to use "judicial construction" to place or infer limits on legislative statutes. The function of the courts was to "enforce the legislative will," not determine what that will was. "To limit this statute in the manner now asked for would be to make a new law, not enforce an old one. This is no part of our duty." Therefore, Waite concluded, Congress had "not as yet provided by appropriate legislation" punishment for the crimes with which the defendants had been charged. If the statutes were bad, so too were indictments based on them. The Circuit Court was correct in sustaining the demurrers to the indictments and rendering judgment in favor of Hiram Reese and the others.

Justice Clifford's concurring opinion, more than twice as long as the chief justice's, agreed that the indictment was bad, but for reasons "widely different from those assigned by the court." There is no reason to doubt that Clifford's concurrence was much the same opinion he had originally drafted for the Court at Waite's request, which was rejected later by the justices at their November 27 meeting. The opinion also seemed to justify Waite's confidence in Clifford's fascination, if not expertise, with "penal statutes." For Clifford the indictments were "faulty" not because they were based on a faulty statute, but because the indictments "did not accurately and clearly describe all the ingredients of which the offence is composed." Hiram Reese and the others were wrongfully convicted not because of their alleged denial of William Garner's offer to vote on account of Garner's race, but because the indictments did not show that Garner was "otherwise qualified" to vote. In other words, it was more important for Clifford that the government show that Garner could vote than that he had been prevented from doing so.

Clifford essentially agreed that the Fifteenth Amendment and the Enforcement Acts were intended to eliminate disabilities to vote of "every kind arising from race, color or previous condition of servitude." That authority was limited only to disabilities involving race. Other prerequisites for voting remained the states' prerogative, and these applied equally to both races. Unless a black voter was so "otherwise qualified" to vote, "he is no more entitled to enjoy that privilege than a white male citizen who does not possess the qualifications required by law." According to the Lexington law, a citizen had to meet certain residency requirements and pay the capitation tax of $1.50 "on or before the 15th of January preceding the election" to qualify to vote in the city election. From the very beginning Clifford had seemed fixated on the question of the Garner's payment of the tax. On his copy of the briefs he had noted alongside of the listing of the counts of the indictment, "Bad. Does not allege that he paid the capitation tax." In his opinion Clifford returns to this problem again and again. Did Garner's "offer" to pay the tax as evidenced by his presentation of an "affidavit" to do so on January 30, the day of the election, constitute "performance" that would have then made him "otherwise qualified" to vote? In that case his denial of the vote might have constituted a violation of the statute as drafted. For Clifford the affidavit only provided evidence that Garner had made the offer to pay, but it did not prove Garner's ability to actually pay the tax. That was crucial, for "where the party making the offer is not ready to pay . . . and has then and there the means to make the payment," the denial of the right to vote cannot be charged to "the wrongful act or omission of the person or officer to whom the offer is made."

Although he never explicitly stated so, Clifford assumed that Garner was neither "ready" nor had the "means" to actually pay the tax on January 30. Since the tax had not been paid by the required date, and since the "offer" to pay it on the thirtieth was not sufficient to constitute the fulfilment of the state requirement, Garner was not "otherwise qualified" to vote. Since he was not qualified, the indictments against the defendants were therefore "too vague, uncertain, and indefinite" in their allegations to sustain a conviction. Although historical hindsight is tricky business, it is important to examine two of Clifford's underlying assumptions that he spent so much effort and verbiage to develop.

He assumed that Garner had not fulfilled the prerequisites for qualification for voting, because the law required him to do so by the fifteenth. Garner's "offer" to pay was on the thirtieth. In this Clifford must have been confused by a possible discrepancy in the indictment. On page three of the indictment, under the third count, it alleged that William Garner "did on the 15th day of January, eighteen hundred and seventy three . . . offer to pay said James F. Robinson, Jr. aforesaid Collector, at his office in said city, to pay any capitation tax due from him." It further went on to state that Robinson "then and there wrongfully refused on account of his race or color" to give Garner "any opportunity" to pay the tax. As mentioned before, the indictment was a printed form, and the date of the offer to pay on the fifteenth was filled in. On the following page, in count four, it alleged that on the "30th day of January" Garner did offer "to pay" the capitation tax to Robinson, who "wrongfully refused" to accept the payment. Significantly, the count also included the charge that at the same time Robinson "did then and there give citizens of the white race" the opportunity to pay the tax!

There are two possible interpretations of this, neither of which supports Clifford's assumption. One possibility is that the second date filled in, the "30th" was a mistake, and should have been entered as the "15th" as in the prior count. But that would have indicated that Garner had attempted to fulfill all the requirements for voting "in accordance with the law." The other more likely inference was that both dates were correct, and that having failed to have his tax payment accepted on the fifteenth, which was the last day, he waited again until election day, when he, evidently along with others "of the white race," attempted to pay the tax in order to vote. Indeed, the fourth count does refer to Garner's meeting the residency and age qualifications "at the time of said election." In other words, Garner made at least two attempts to pay the tax. It also seems clear that Clifford's assumption that Garner had neither the ability nor the "means" to actually pay the tax was more wishful thinking (racism?) than common sense. Given the publicity surrounding the election and law, and the political situation, it seems highly unlikely that Garner, or any black voter in Lexington in January of 1873, would have appeared and attempted to pay the tax had he not had sufficient funds to do so.

By drawing such close attention to the language and content of the indictments, Clifford's opinion also raises a small mystery about this case. In all counts of the indictment James F. Robinson Jr. was identified as the official responsible for assessing and collecting the capitation tax. In count three the grand jury found that he had "wrongfully" denied Garner's offer to pay the tax on January 15. More importantly, count four specifically alleged that on November 30 he had not only refused Garner's offer, but had done so presumably based on Garner's race, since the count alleged that he accepted the payment of "white men." Unfortunately, the record is silent on why he was named but not charged as one of the "co-conspirators." The indictment explicitly accused Robinson of racial discrimination in the performance of his duty, yet was silent on that same account when it came to Reese and the others.

It was left to Justice Ward Hunt in his lone, and lengthy, dissent to remind the Supreme Court, and perhaps the nation as well, that *U.S. v. Reese* was about something more than statutory construction and the linguistic subtleties of framing indictments. Indeed, he expressed his frustration with the Court's majority and the fact that the "particularity in an indictment or in the statutory description of offences has at times been extreme, the distinctions almost ridiculous." He added that sometimes "good sense is sacrificed to technical nicety, and a sound principle carried to an extravagant extent." Attempting to restore some of that missing good sense, Hunt conscientiously challenged each of the majority's conclusions and discussed what they, perhaps too often conveniently, had left out. This was certainly the case with the majority's finding that sections 3 and 4 of the May 1870 Enforcement Act were insufficient because they did not include the words "on account of race" as an element of the wrongful actions of an election official. According to Hunt the Court's majority had ignored both the language and the "intent" of Congress in passing the legislation. Hunt found that intent "too plain to discuss," but he did nonetheless. He pointed out that in the Senate debates on the legislation the same question that had troubled Waite had been raised. Was it necessary, it had been asked, to include the phrase "on account of race" in sections 3 and 4, especially since the first two sections of the act did explicitly use those words? Supporters of the legislation argued that the language of the third and fourth sections did "embrace" the same "class of cases" as the first two sections, that is, wrongful refusals on account of race. Moreover, Congress did provide an explicit link between the sections when it inserted the words "as aforesaid" in sections 3 and 4 in qualifying the elements of wrongful denial or hindrance of voters or votes. The actions of an official under sections 3 and 4 were wrongful by reason of the act "aforesaid." For both Congress and Hunt, that term had to refer to an act done, or not done, "on account of race," as stated in the first two sections. "By the words 'as aforesaid,' the provisions respecting race and color of the first and second sections of the statute are incorporated into and made a part of the third and fourth sections." Lest he be accused of verbal nitpicking himself, Hunt noted that unless construed this way, the words "as aforesaid" would be "wholly and absolutely without meaning." They must refer to something, otherwise why would Congress have used them? If Congress had intended to prevent wrongful actions of officials on account of race as stated in the first two sections, then the words "hindered and prevented his voting as aforesaid" in the fourth section and "wrongfully refused . . . as aforesaid" in the third section were necessary to "sufficiently accomplish this purpose of the statute." For Justice Hunt, the statute was clearly good and did indeed accurately and legally describe the crimes for which the defendants were charged.

Hunt likewise had little patience with Clifford's parsing of the language of the indictments. The purpose of an indictment, Hunt argued, was to "appraise" the court and the defendant of the crime or crimes charged. While the "strict construction" of a statute might be expected in an indictment, it is not always so. The language of an indictment should not be held to such a particular standard that it excludes what the legislature intended to accomplish by the statute. If a class of persons or actions is defined by a statute, it should not be the role of the courts to exclude a particular act or person if they fit the overall intent of the legislature. This "liberal rule" of construction is especially necessary where, as in the present case, the form of the statute is penal, but the broader intent "is in fact to protect freedom." In this, Hunt mirrored the chief justice's warning that judges are not supposed to make the law or fix legislative mistakes. For Waite, the Court should not presume to second-guess the language of a statute; for Hunt, judges should not presume to ignore the intent behind the language. Hunt also took the opportunity to point out to the penal-statute expert on the Court, Justice Clifford, that in fact a "well-settled principle" of criminal proceedings in federal courts was that a conviction based on an indictment with both good and bad counts would be sustained.

Hunt concluded that "the indictment is sufficient, and the statute sufficiently describes the offence." He didn't stop there. Indeed, Hunt reserved his strongest objections for what the Court majority *didn't* discuss. Despite all the discussion and analysis of statutes and indictments, nowhere did the Court deal with the real underlying issue presented in the case, the meaning and intent of the Fifteenth Amendment and the constitutionality of the Enforcement Act of May 1870. It seemed that the Court had done everything to step around the issue, so Justice Hunt took the opportunity to essentially remind his brethren of what had been going on in the country over the past ten years. The Fifteenth Amendment had been "the third of a series of amendments intended to protect the rights of the newly emancipated freedmen of the South." The Thirteenth Amendment had abolished slavery and was the "first and the great step" toward "the protection and confirmation of the political rights" of the former slaves. Congressional adoption of the Fourteenth Amendment was "another strong measure in the same direction," but it was not enough. It still left a "large colored population in the Southern States, lately slaves and necessarily ignorant" without the real means to protect themselves. The Fifteenth Amendment was the tool Congress gave the freedpeople to do this, by conferring upon them "all the political rights possessed by the white inhabitants of the State." Echoing the earlier arguments of Frederick Douglass and Congressman George Boutwell, Hunt stated the freedpeople "could be most effectively secured in the protection of their rights of life, liberty, and the pursuit of happiness, by giving them the greatest of rights among freemen—the ballot." While Hunt did not go so far as to explicitly contradict Waite's dictum that the Fifteenth Amendment did not give anyone the right to vote, he suggested that while the amendment "expressly" negated state denials or abridgements of the "right to vote," it also must be read to mean the "right to vote in the broadest terms."

Hunt had no doubt that the Enforcement Act was constitutional. Even without section 2 of the amendment, giving Congress authority to pass "appropriate legislation," Congress had that authority. Hunt cited earlier Supreme Court decisions, such as the *McCulloch v. Maryland* bank case of 1819, and the more recent *Legal Tender Cases*, both of which involved a "broad" interpretation of congressional authority based on the "necessary and proper" clause of the Constitution. If Congress decided that the "necessities of the country" required the establishment of a national bank or the issuance of legal-tender notes, then that judgment was "conclusive on the court . . . and not within their power to review it." If Congress then "desires to protect the freedman in his rights as a citizen and voter" against those who are "prejudiced and unscrupulous in their hostility to him and his newly conferred rights," they could certainly do so. Congress was not prohibited from passing penal statutes to protect the rights of citizens. According to Hunt, the statute books of all countries "abound" with law punishing those who violate or infringe on the rights of others. In what was as close to impassioned as a nineteenth-century Supreme Court justice was likely to get, Hunt wrote:

Punishment is the means; protection is the end. The arrest conviction, and sentence to imprisonment, of one inspector, who refused the vote of a person of African descent on account of his race, would more effectively secure the right of the voter than would any number of civil suits in the State courts, prosecuted by timid, ignorant, penniless parties against those possessing the wealth, influence, and the sentiment of the community.

Hunt had not finished. In an argument that at that time may have seemed far less ironic than it does today, he "proved" the enforcement legislation was also constitutional by reason of Article 4, Section 5, of the Constitution, the so-called fugitive slave clause. According to Hunt, this section authorized Congress to "protect the rights of the slaveholder in his slaves." In order to enforce this protection Congress had passed a series of laws over the years "providing not only the means of restoring the escaped slave to his master, but inflicting punishment upon those who violated the master's rights." Hunt cited the Supreme Court's rulings in *Prigg v. Pennsylvania* and *Ableman v. Booth* upholding the constitutionality of such legislation. The Court based its rulings on the doctrine that the national government, even in the absence of "positive provisions," is bound through its own "legislative, executive, and judicial" departments to carry into effect all the "rights and duties" imposed by the Constitution. The constitutional provisions protecting the freedmen, like that protecting the slaveholders, are part of the national Constitution, and as such "provides the means of enforcing its authority, through fines and imprisonment, in the federal courts." For Hunt, the Enforcement Act was entirely "legal."

Dissenting opinions in constitutional jurisprudence have no legal force, except to possibly point the way for future Court majorities to modify or reverse their rulings. It is the majority opinion (or opinions as in *Reese*) that determines the actual outcome of a case before the Supreme Court, and so it is perhaps understandable that Hunt's dissent was pretty much ignored at the time, and since. It may well be that Hunt's six-year tenure on the Court was too brief to develop a reputation, as his soon-to-be fellow justice John Marshall Harlan would, as the "great dissenter" in the name of protecting civil rights. Moreover, Harlan was a southerner and former slaveholder himself. Hunt's views were more predictable, given his New York Republican background. Conversion stories make much better reading.

Nonetheless, Hunt's dissenting opinion does merit attention. At the very least, it was the brief that Attorney General Williams and Solicitor General Phillips should have submitted on behalf of the government, but didn't. Hunt's opinion also highlighted what the majority didn't say or do in *Reese*, and the essential moderation of the Court's majority ruling. Presumably, the Court had found sections 3 and 4 of the 1870 Enforcement Act unconstitutional. But nowhere did the Court say so in plain terms. What Waite did say was that the sections were not "sufficient." Did that mean the same as "unconstitutional"? If so, it would have been the first time the Court had used the prior term to refer to the latter. Moreover, even assuming the Supreme Court had found the two sections unconstitutional, did that nullify the entire 1870 act, let alone the other subsequent enforcement statutes? Hunt's opinion also called attention to that silence. Finally, Hunt's reading of the Reconstruction Amendments, and congressional authority to implement them, clearly reflected the strong Republican nationalist sentiment of the immediate post– Civil War years. This sentiment recognized not only the sovereignty of the federal government, but also the responsibility of that government to protect the political and civil rights of the freedpeople. Stating these views highlighted the Court's refusal to completely abandon this position. While the majority in *Reese* did not accept this strong nationalist position, neither did it accept the extreme states' rights constitutionalism urged by the defendants' attorneys. In light of Hunt's dissent, even Waite's most definitive statement that the Fifteenth Amendment did not give any one the "right to vote" was, in context, irrelevant. Nowhere in the majority opinion in *Reese* did the Court reject national authority to protect voters from discrimination based on race.

This moderation in regard to the relationship between the federal government and the states was even more obvious in Waite's opinion in *U.S. v. Cruikshank*. Writing for a unanimous Court, Waite's opinion essentially consisted of two sections: the first involved a discussion of federalism, while the second focused on the

{ *Reconstruction and Black Suffrage* }

various counts of the indictment. According to the chief justice, each citizen of the United States is subject to two governments: the government of the United States and "a government of each of the several states." This makes each citizen subject to two sets of government, and each government is responsible for protecting that citizen's rights "within its jurisdiction." Using this distinction of "dual citizenship" developed recently by the Court in the *Slaughterhouse Cases*, Waite conceded that a person may be a citizen both of the United States and of a state, "but his rights of citizenship under one of these governments will be different from those he has under the other."

Waite, however, was careful not to carry this concept of "dual citizenship" further than necessary toward the states' rights side of the argument. He noted that the people of the United States "required" a national government for national purposes. Back in 1789, when the "separate States" found that the "articles of confederation . . . were not sufficient," the "people of the United States . . . ordained and established the government of the United States." This was a crucial admission because in the years prior to the Civil War, one of the basic premises of the states' rights theory of the Constitution had been that the Constitution was created by, and therefore subject to, the "separate states," and not the "people" as Waite now stated. Moreover, the powers of the national government are limited in number "but not in degree," and within the scope of its powers "it is supreme and above the states."

Waite then described the practical implication of this "dual federalism." A person residing in a state is subject to two governments, but there is necessarily "no conflict" between the powers each has over the individual, since these governments have been established for "different purposes" and "have separate jurisdictions." Yet this is not always the case. Sometimes it happens that "a person is amenable to both jurisdictions for one and the same act." As an example the chief justice cited the case of a U.S. marshal who, in attempting to exercise the process of the court within a state, faces an unlawful resistance accompanied by an assault. In that instance, the "sovereignty of the United States is violated by the resistance, and that of the State by the breach of the peace, in the assault." He also cited as example the passing of "counterfeited coin of the United States." Such an act would be a federal offense because it "discredits" United States currency and a state offense because of the "fraud upon him to whom it is passed."

If a citizen is subject to both governments, and if, in Waite's words, he "owes allegiance" to both governments, what can he expect in return? "In return," Waite concluded, "he can demand protection from each within its own jurisdiction." This would seem both obvious and circular. Who is the protection for and from what? Apparently, what is protected are a citizen's rights. That led back to the original question:what are those rights so protected? The rights protected by the federal government, Waite answered, were only those rights "acquired under the Constitution or laws of the United States." All other rights are "left under the protection of the states." At this point, the chief justice's argument took a fateful turn. He avoided any mention of section 6 of the Enforcement Act and whether or not the section, or the entire act, represented those rights subject to federal protection. Instead Waite went back to the indictments. The issue to be decided in this case, according to the chief justice, was thus narrowed from the outset to an "examination of the indictments," *not* the legislation on which they were based. Rather than examine the law, the Court decided to use the indictments in order to "ascertain" whether the rights that the defendants were alleged to have interfered with "are such as had been in law and in fact granted or secured by the constitution or laws of the United States."

The "several rights" the defendants allegedly violated were the same four presented by their attorneys' briefs. They included the right to peacefully assemble from the First Amendment; the right to bear arms from the Second Amendment; and the Fourteenth and Fifteenth Amendments. The remainder of Waite's opinion considered the specific counts of the indictment as they related to each of these rights in turn. This section of Waite's opinion was for the most part a summary of the arguments presented in the defendants' briefs. With respect to the claims regarding the First and Second Amendments, the chief justice relied on the Supreme Court's 1835 ruling in *Barron v. Baltimore.* In that case the Court held that the Bill of Rights was a limit on the federal government only. Whether this was still the case, especially in light of the Fourteenth Amendment, was beside the point for Waite. According to the chief justice, "It is now too late to question the correctness of this construction." The First Amendment "assumes" the existence of the right of the people "to assemble for lawful purposes, and protects it against encroachments by Congress." The amendment did not create this right, it only prohibited Congress from interfering with it. For their "protection in its enjoyment" citizens had to look to their states. "The power for that purpose was originally placed there and it has never been surrendered to the United States." Therefore, the two counts of the indictment that charged the defendants with hindering and preventing citizens from assembly together for a "peaceful and lawful purpose" were improper because they stated no federally protected right.

Then Waite made a remarkable concession. There was a federally protected right connected to peaceful assembly and the First Amendment. It involved the right of the people to assemble "for the purpose of petitioning Congress for a redress of grievances." This right, which was based on "the very idea of government, republican in form," allowed citizens to meet peacefully "for consultation in respect to public affairs, and for a redress of grievances." It was also among the federally protected privileges and immunities that had been recognized by the Supreme Court in the *Slaughterhouse Cases.* If the two counts in the indictment had alleged that the defendants had intended to hinder and prevent a meeting for this particular purpose, as opposed to "any lawful purpose," "the case would have been within the statute, and within the scope of the sovereignty of the United States." In other words, the two counts had been phrased incorrectly. Waite's objection to the two counts of the indictment relating to the Second Amendment were also premised on the *Barron* ruling. The defendants were said to have violated the right of "bearing arms for a lawful purpose." However, the right to bear arms was not a right granted by the Constitution. Like freedom of assembly, the right to bear arms could not be infringed by the national government. For protection against violations of that right the people had to look to the "police" powers of their state governments.

"More objectionable" to the Court were the counts of the indictment based on the Fourteenth and Fifteenth Amendments. The Fourteenth Amendment "adds nothing to the rights of one citizen as against another." It merely prohibited the states from infringing on those "fundamental rights" that belong to all citizens. The two counts of the indictment alleging a "conspiracy" to "falsely imprison and murder citizens of the United States" referred not to federally protected rights, but to rights that were part of those "unalienable rights" whose protection "rests alone with the states." For the Court it was no more the duty of the federal government, or within its power, to prohibit "conspiracy" to murder or falsely imprison than it would be to punish false imprisonment or murder "itself." Equally insufficient were the counts of the indictment charging the defendants with preventing and hindering "citizens of African descent and persons of color" from the "free exercise" of the enjoyment of their rights as citizens. The problem here, for the chief justice, was not federal authority to provide such protections, but the indictment's making "no allegation" that the actions taken by the defendants were done "because of the race or color of the persons conspired against." When stripped of their "verbiage," Waite concluded, the counts did nothing more than allege that "certain citizens" had been denied the equal protection of the laws, and this was certainly not within the meaning of the Fourteenth Amendment.

The chief justice used this same reasoning to attack those counts relating to the Fifteenth Amendment. Citing the just-announced decision in *Reese* and the Court's ruling in *Minor v. Happersett*. Waite reiterated the dictum that the Fifteenth Amendment had not "conferred" suffrage upon anyone. But the amendment did invest citizens with a "new" constitutional right that could be protected by the federal government, the "exemption from discrimination in the exercise of the elective franchise on account of race, color, or previous condition of servitude."

The right to vote comes from the states, but the right to be ex- empt from racial discrimination in the exercise of that right is an "attribute of national citizenship . . . secured by the Constitution of the United States."

In what would become one of the most quoted passages from his *Cruikshank* opinion, the chief justice ruled that the charges that the defendants had unlawfully hindered and prevented the "citizens named, being of African descent and colored," from ex- ercising their "several and respective right and privilege to vote" were invalid because the indictment did not allege that the de- fendants did so on account of race:

> Inasmuch, therefore, as it does not appear in these counts that the intent of the defendants was to prevent these parties from exercising their right to vote on account of their race &c., it does not appear that it was their intent to interfere with any right granted or secured by the constitution or the laws of the United States. *We may suspect that race was the cause of the hostility, but it is not so averred.* This is material to a description of the substance of the offence, and cannot be supplied by im- plication. Everything essential must be charged positively, not inferentially. The defect here is not in form, but in substance.

The chief justice completed his opinion and the demolition of the indictment by applying the same reasoning to all remaining counts of the indictment. All were "too vague and uncertain" to provide the defendants their own constitutional rights under the Fourth Amendment, that is, to be informed of the nature and cause of the crimes with which they were charged. Waite cited a number of analogies to show how the omission from indictment that Levi Nelson and Alexander Tillman (and the dozens of oth- ers killed in Grant Parish that day) were victimized "on account of their race" meant that the indictments themselves lacked the "certainty and precision required by the established rules of criminal pleading." He argued, for example, that it is a crime to steal goods and chattels, but an indictment for such a crime would be bad if it did not "specify with some degree of certainty the articles stolen." All of the charges that involved the crime of "conspiracy" were likewise found insufficient "in law" to provide defendants with the opportunity to adequately defend themselves. As a result the Supreme Court ruled that the counts of the indictment against Cruikshank and the others was "so defective that no judgement of conviction should be pronounced upon them." The Court affirmed the circuit court's order in arrest of the trial court's judgment, and directed that the defendants be "discharged."

The remarkable thing about the Supreme Court's decision in *Cruikshank* is that, stripped of its "verbiage," it was even more narrow in its result than *Reese*. The *Cruikshank* Court had merely found that the indictments, not (as in *Reese*) the relevant sections of the Enforcement Act on which they were based, were "not sufficient." In that regard the decision clearly followed Bradley's circuit court ruling, and to some extent Clifford's concerns in his concurring opinion in *Reese*. However, it ignored the issue of the constitutionality of the Enforcement Act entirely. Moreover, despite Waite's claim in *Reese* that the Fifteenth Amendment did not grant anyone the right to vote, the two decisions did recognize two important points. Both decisions agreed that the Fifteenth Amendment did protect citizens from voter discrimination based on race. Both decisions also clearly and explicitly confirmed congressional authority to protect that right from discrimination based on race. When it came to the First and Second Amendments, the Supreme Court had left the federal system much as it had been before 1865. The Court's acceptance of the process of "incorporating" the protections of the Bill of Rights to the states using the Fourteenth Amendment would not appear until the 1920s. However, the Court in *Reese* and *Cruikshank* was far less supportive of the defendants' claims that the Fourteenth and Fifteenth Amendments had been equally insignificant in changing the equation of power between the national government and the states.

Whatever the general constitutional issues argued and decided in a Supreme Court decision, the Court's primary function is to review and rule on the specific cases before it. In *U.S. v. Reese* and

U.S. v. Cruikshank this meant the Court had to rule on the specific motions that had brought the cases before the Court. Both cases had been appealed to the Supreme Court, based on a "division" between the circuit court judges hearing the case. In both cases, the Court affirmed the circuit court rulings that overturned the convictions of the defendants. In *Reese* the division between the circuit court judges had been over a demurrer to the indictments made by defendants' counsel. In *Cruikshank* the division between Judge Woods and Justice Bradley had been over the defense motion to "arrest judgement." These motions were different in terms of timing and legal procedure. The immediate result of their affirmation by the Supreme Court was the same. On March 27, 1875, Hiram Reese, William Cruikshank, and their fellow defendants were all free men.

CHAPTER 7

"A Free Ballot and a Fair Count"

To judge from the press, the public's response to the Supreme Court's rulings in *Reese* and *Cruikshank* was overwhelmingly positive. The staunchly Republican *New York Times* enthused over the "admirable clearness and emphasis of the opinions." The *Times* reprinted both decisions in full, except for Hunt's dissenting and Clifford's concurring opinions in *Reese*. Indeed, most of its praise was directed at the Court's opinion in the Kentucky case. And while earlier the newspaper had described the Grant Parish massacre as a "fiendish deed," it now decided that the Supreme Court's ruling on the convictions of those responsible was "not so important" as the other case, except as a warning to future prosecuting attorneys that their indictments must be drawn "with the utmost possible regard for the rights of all concerned." Papers around the country expressed similar sentiments, and joined with the *Chicago Tribune* in congratulating the new chief justice on a pair of opinions that had certainly earned him the "confidence of his countrymen." As expected, Democratic and southern newspapers were even more enthusiastic about the Court's ruling and their praise of Waite. One paper now compared him to great chief justices of the past like John Marshall and Roger B. Taney, and the *Richmond Enquirer* praised Waite "on the utterances worthy of the fathers." The press was equally certain that the decisions marked a new era in the relations between Washington and the states, and between north and south generally. The decisions' implications for African Americans were less emphasized, although the *New Orleans Times* suggested that "the colored suffragan, if not already conscious of the fact, must know that his prerogatives, under the constitution as amended, are no greater than those of any other citizen."

The chief justice had been apprehensive about the response to the Court's opinions in these cases. Judge Hugh Lennox Bond, a Grant appointee from Maryland who did circuit court duty with Waite, had referred to the case as "that 'Dred' decision of the enforcement case," bringing to mind the earlier notorious Court ruling on slavery, *Dred Scott v. Sandford*. Waite admitted that the cases had been troubling and "cost me a heap of hard work" and that the "past few weeks have borne upon me." But he was gratified at the favorable comments he had received in the press, especially Republican papers like the *Times*, which now decided that his appointment to the chief justiceship was a "judicious one, adding strength and dignity to the great tribunal over which he presides."

Whatever the papers at the time may or may not have understood, the Court's rulings in *Reese* and *Cruikshank* were victories for opponents of voting rights in only a narrow legal sense, or a broadly symbolic one. Only three sections of only one of four enforcement measures were found unconstitutional. If anyone thought these two cases had determined once and for all the fate of the Enforcement Acts of 1870–71, and marked an end to the federal government's role in protecting franchise rights, they were probably disappointed. The bulk of enforcement legislation remained on the books, and two months after the decisions were announced Congress repassed the two sections voided in *Reese*. The two new sections, 5506 and 5507, of what were now known as the Revised Statutes, were more specific than the earlier sections voided by the Court, but were still based on "the right of suffrage, to whom that right is guaranteed by the fifteenth Amendment." Moreover, the remainder of the May 1871 legislation, dealing with the machinery of enforcement and the jurisdiction of federal officials and courts, and even the provisions authorizing the president to use federal troops or militias to assist enforcement, likewise remained on the books. Though large parts of the election laws were eventually repealed by Congress in 1893, sections 5506 to 5532 remained the law through the end of the century.

Along with a series of lower federal court and Supreme Court rulings in the years immediately following, the two cases suggested that the judiciary had clearly not abandoned the idea of national authority over the electoral process, nor completely abandoned the Republican commitment to political equality for the freedpeople. Indeed, that authority was consistently sustained. What did change was the constitutional rationale behind that authority and the political context of its actual implementation. In 1878, in the case *In re Goldman*, Judge William B. Woods, sitting again on the circuit court in Louisiana, upheld the power of the federal government to punish anyone intimidating voters at a federal election. According to Woods, Article I, Section 2, of the Constitution itself gave Congress the "ultimate power" of protecting voters making their choice, or "afterwards expressing their choice," at an election in which members of Congress were to be elected. A voter otherwise qualified to vote by state laws, Woods concluded, derived his right to vote for congressmen from the Constitution. Therefore, Congress had the power to protect him in that right.

This was certainly a new idea, or at least one that had not appeared or been used in any of the judicial proceedings involving the Enforcement Acts up to this time. And Congress had made no mention of the applicability of the laws to congressional elections when it considered the revised statutes. Where then did the idea originate for using the constitutional provision dealing with Congress's authority over the "times, places, and manner" of holding elections to sustain the election laws? To some extent the idea had been implied in Waite's *Cruikshank* opinion. His acceptance of the "dual" nature of federalism and citizenship recognized that when it came to the protection of "national" rights or "delegated powers" of the national government, the government could certainly do so. Another possibility is that it originated with the Department of Justice. In September of 1876, just prior to the presidential elections, Alphonso Taft, President Grant's fifth and final attorney general, issued a crcular letter of instructions to United States marshals throughout the country as to their duties in the upcoming election. In preparing the document Taft noted that he had "considered recent important judgements by the Supreme Court . . . upon the acts of Congress which regulate this general topic" and concluded that those judgments "do not concern elections for Federal offices." Taft ordered federal marshals to preserve the "peace of the United States" and secure voters against whatever hindered or prevented them from the "free exercise of the elective franchise." And he reminded the marshals that the laws of the United States are "supreme" and that "no state law or official" had the authority or "jurisdiction" to oppose or hinder them in their duties.

A year after Wood's ruling the Supreme Court confronted the constitutionality of the revised election laws in the companion cases of *Ex parte Siebold* and *Ex parte Clark*. The cases involved the convictions of Maryland and Ohio state election officials, stemming from the 1878 congressional elections. The officials were charged with a variety of illegal acts, including stuffing ballot boxes, failing to deliver ballot boxes to the county clerk for counting, and allowing ballot boxes to be opened and the ballots destroyed. Speaking for a unanimous Court, Justice Bradley upheld the constitutionality of all of the sections of the revised statutes, including those sections of the later Enforcement Acts involving the appointment of special election supervisors and deputy marshals in places with twenty thousand or more citizens. The Court took the opportunity to revisit the jurisdictional issue with regard to federal versus state regulation of elections in general. Counsel for the defendants had argued that since voter qualifications came from the states, any conflicts arising out of federal attempts to regulate elections and voting should be decided in favor of the states. Bradley rejected this line of reasoning, concluding that congressional regulations "are paramount to those made by the state legislatures; and if they conflict therewith, the latter, so far as the conflict extends, ceases to be operative."

In justifying this result the Court applied a doctrine drawn from its 1837 ruling in *Cooley v. Board of Wardens* involving the distinctions between federal and state authority over interstate commerce. In *Cooley* the Court held that in some area of commerce where no federal legislation existed, the states were free to regulate on their own. But once Congress did act, if there was a conflict with state regulations, federal legislation was "paramount." This notion of "concurrent authority" was now applied to federal election laws, at least to those elections that involved a "national interest," such as those for members of Congress. Moreover, the Court rejected defendants' claims that such federal legislation, even if valid, could apply only to private individuals and not those officials acting in their official capacity as representatives of the state. This was of course the reverse of the defendants' argument in *Reese*, and the Court would have none of it. "A violation of duty is an offence against the United States for which the offender is justly amenable to that government. No official position can shelter him from this responsibility."

Between 1880 and 1883 a series of lower federal court rulings applied and expanded on these cases. In *U.S. v. Mumford*, the circuit court in Virginia confronted a situation similar to that in Kentucky. In 1876 the Virginia state legislature had passed a law requiring payment of a poll tax as a prerequisite for voting in the state. The law was widely unpopular because it prevented many poor whites from voting as well as blacks, and was eventually repealed in 1882. However, before, during, and after the November 1882 elections it was used to disfranchise thousands of African-American voters. Robert Mumford, a Democratic tax commissioner, was accused of conspiracy to prevent voters in the Third Congressional District of Virginia from voting by his failure to assess and collect the tax.

Mumford was indicted and convicted under section 5506 of the Revised Statutes, and his appeal was heard before federal circuit court judge Hugh Bond and district court judge Robert Hughes. Hughes had run unsuccessfully as the Republican candidate for governor of Virginia in 1873, and at the time of his appointment by President Grant to the federal bench he served as a federal district attorney in Virginia. Both Hughes and Bond were among a group of southern judges in the lower federal courts who during this time consistently, and courageously, supported equal rights and protection for African Americans. At his appeal Mumford's attorneys argued that section 5506 was unconstitutional, citing the Supreme Court's ruling in *Reese*. In separate concurring opinions both Bond and Hughes rejected this claim. Pointing to the legislative history of section 5506, both judges emphasized how Congress had taken the sections of the Enforcement Act of 1871 voided in *Reese* and eliminated all reference to the Fifteenth Amendment and racial discrimination. Instead Congress based the revised sections on the fourth section of Article I of the Constitution, which gave Congress authority over "the times, places, and manner of holding elections" in elections at which federal officials were to be chosen. In upholding Mumford's conviction, and the constitutionality of the federal laws, Judge Bond suggested that the critical distinction between the present case and *Reese* was that the latter involved a municipal election. Had the crimes been committed at a federal election, Bond believed, the Court in *Reese* would have most likely upheld the indictments.

By far the most important affirmation of federal authority over the electoral process and voting came in the Supreme Court's 1884 decision in *Ex parte Yarbrough*. As in *Cruikshank*, the case involved Klan-type activity against African Americans. In October 1883 a number of persons were indicted by a federal grand jury in Banks County, Georgia, charged with the "most cruel outrages" against the "colored people" of the area. The attacks were presumably in retaliation for their Republican votes in the preceding November congressional elections. Among those indicted were several members of the family of Jasper Yarbrough. The family was part of a Democratic organization known as the "Pop and Go Club," and although at the trial an attempt was made to show that this group was merely a baseball club, it was obvious that it was essentially a Klan organization whose real purpose was to wreak terror and vengeance on blacks and any other political enemies. It was shown that during the summer of 1883 the "Club" made numerous night "excursions" throughout the countryside, dragging blacks out of their homes, beating and whipping them, and in at least once instance, shooting and killing a black man.

Speaking for a unanimous Court, Justice Miller affirmed the conviction of Jasper Yarbrough and his brothers. Significantly, unlike *Cruikshank*, where the Court focused on the specific laws in question, in *Yarbrough* the Supreme Court seemed less interested in the specific sections of the revised statutes than in Congress's authority to pass such laws. This power, Miller concluded, was both necessary and considerable. "If this government is anything more than a mere aggregation of delegated agents of the other States and governments, each of which is superior to the General Government, it must have the power to protect the elections on which its existence depends from violence and corruption." Justice Miller traced over three-quarters of a century's worth of congressional measures intended to "remedy more than one evil" arising from the election of congressmen at different times and in different states. Conceding that most of this legislation involved the "times and places" of federal elections, Miller had "no doubt" that authority for regulating the "manner and conduct" of such elections was equally within the national government's purview. That it hadn't done so before was merely a matter of "deference and respect" to the states. Miller also gave short shrift to the objections raised by defendants' counsel that even if Congress had the authority to regulate the conduct of federal elections, that authority extended only to attacks or violations against public officials, and not against private citizens as charged in the indictment. The Court found no distinction between the two, and congressional authority to protect one included the power to protect both. Preventing the "adverse influence of force and fraud" extended to both officials and those "electors" who have the right to take part in elections.

Significantly, Justice Miller and the Court chose to look once more at a crucial issue that supposedly had been settled eight years earlier in *Reese* and *Cruikshank*. The Yarbroughs' attorneys had argued that since qualifications for voting were determined by the states, it followed that the right to vote itself came from the states. As support they relied on the Supreme Court's 1874 ruling in *Minor v. Happersett*, in which the Court upheld a Missouri election-registering officer's refusal to allow Virginia L. Minor to vote, on the grounds that she was a woman. Speaking in the *Minor* case for a unanimous court, Chief Justice Waite determined that suffrage was not among the "privileges and immunities" of United States citizenship as defined by the Fourteenth

Amendment. States were therefore within their authority to exclude women from the franchise, even as some states had by then included them. The Constitution, Waite concluded, "does not confer the right of suffrage upon any one" and state constitutions and laws that "commit that important trust to men alone are not necessarily void."

The chief justice had said much the same thing nine years earlier in *Reese* when he held that the "Fifteenth Amendment does not confer the right of suffrage upon any one." It would thus have been expected for the Court to follow that premise in *Yarbrough*. But it didn't. Indeed, Justice Miller, in effect, seriously qualified the earlier ruling, ruling that "under some circumstances" the Fifteenth Amendment was the source of an immediate right to vote on the part of African Americans. To the question of what were such circumstances, Miller answered that "in all cases where the former slaveholding states had not removed from the Constitutions the words 'white man' as a qualification for voting" the Fifteenth Amendment and the subsequent congressional legislation did confer a positive grant of suffrage. Since the amendment and the legislation were "paramount" to state laws, their effect was to annul the discriminating word "white" and in effect grant blacks the same voting rights as white men. Using a Latin legal term meaning "by its own force," Miller concluded that the Fifteenth Amendment "does, *propio vigore*, substantially confer in the negro the right to vote, and Congress has the power to protect and enforce that right."

These post-*Reese* decisions would seem confusing, supporting as they do the very national authority restricted in 1875. Had the Supreme Court reversed itself within a decade, and if so, what was the status of the federal government's enforcement policy? The answer to both these questions reflects the momentous political developments nationally and in the South that coincided with the Court's response to Republican Reconstruction policies. According to the popular late-nineteenth-century fictional newspaper character Mr. Dooley, the Supreme Court "follows the election returns." That being the case, the line of federal court rulings from *Reese* and *Cruikshank* up through *Yarbrough* in 1884 represents both the Republican Party's "retreat" from its commitment to the civil and political equality of southern blacks and its unwillingness to completely abandon African Americans to their former masters. The mixture of principles and partisan calculation that led to the Fifteenth Amendment and the Enforcement Acts continued after 1875, but in a more restricted context. As Republican regimes in the southern states were overthrown by Democrats, there would be fewer options to protect political rights in the face of attempts by white southerners to restore their racial supremacy by legal or illegal means.

Indeed, the Supreme Court's decisions in *Reese* and *Cruikshank* coincided with an important political turning point in the history of Reconstruction, the presidential election of 1876. Two months after the decision the Republican Party met to choose Grant's successor. It was not going to be an easy choice, since the party was weakened from within by the factionalism of the past four years. The Stalwarts, Mugwumps, and Liberal Republicans all had their own grievances and agendas. The corruption and scandals of the Grant administration had likewise sullied the GOP's image, as had the economic depression of 1873. In response Republicans nominated Ohio governor Rutherford B. Hayes, known for his honesty and integrity and the fact that he "was obnoxious to no one." Sensing opportunity, Democrats chose a northern governor, Samuel Tilden of New York, as their presidential candidate. Tilden was known for his integrity and honesty, and had gained prominence by successfully taming the infamous Tweed Ring in New York City politics. Both party platforms in 1876 stressed economic development and political reform, and both parties acknowledged the obligation to protect the rights of "all men." But the Republicans focused on another theme that had served them in the recent past. The tactic was known as "waving the bloody shirt." It reminded voters that the Democratic Party was the party of secession and four years of terrible conflict, while the Republicans had saved the Union, ended slavery, and promoted equality. Hayes and his supporters warned of the return of "rebel rule" and maintained that true reconciliation between the sections was impossible if the rights of the freedpeople were disregarded.

In fact, the return of "rebel rule" had already begun. By November 1876 all but three states of the former Confederacy had been "redeemed" and were under the political control of white Democrats. Those three states, Louisiana, South Carolina, and Florida, along with Oregon, turned one of the most bitterly fought political campaigns in history into political high drama. Disputed returns from these states following election day meant that neither Hayes nor Tilden had a majority of the electoral votes needed to be declared president. It was an unprecedented situation, since the Twelfth Amendment applied when no candidate received a majority of electoral votes, but not when the votes themselves were in dispute. Eventually, Congress settled on a unique solution to the problem. A fifteen-member electoral commission was created, composed of representatives, senators, and Supreme Court justices, to determine the validity of the returns from the four disputed states. In February 1877, just a month before the scheduled inauguration of the new president, the commission awarded the disputed returns to Hayes. However, the Republican victory came at a price. Under the terms of a purported "bargain" worked out among party leaders at a hotel in New York City, Republicans agreed, among other things, to remove the last federal troops remaining in the South. A month after taking office, Hayes fulfilled that part of the bargain, and symbolically at least, recognized that "rebel rule" had returned to the South, including Louisiana and South Carolina.

The election of 1876, and the so-called Compromise of 1877 that settled the outcome, became the accepted date marking the "end" of Reconstruction and the abandonment of African Americans in the South to their former masters. Yet, like many attempts to set exact dates to a particular historical development or period, such a conclusion obscures as much as it helps in the understanding of what actually occurred. If the Supreme Court was prepared to accept national authority in the protection of at least political rights, so too the Republican Party after 1877 was unwilling to immediately and completely abandon the "promises" of the Reconstruction Amendments, particularly the protection of voting rights. What changed was the rationale behind this continued concern, and the phrase that came to represent this shift was the attempt to protect the "free ballot and a fair count." Of uncertain origin, the phrase appeared more and more in political and governmental sources after 1876. It denoted Republicans' commitment to protect voting rights in the South, but in a partisan rather more than a racial justice sense. Republicans believed that the future of their party in the South depended on political alliance with those elements of the white population, the so-called Bourbons, who shared the increasingly pro-business and economic-development orientation of the party. That this effort would include protecting the rights of the party's most loyal constituency, southern blacks, was certainly recognized, but subsumed under the more racially neutral goal of honest and open elections. Moreover, it could be passed off as a gesture of section conciliation since it also could apply, and was meant to, to all parts of the country. In what would turn out to be a gross mistake, it was hoped that federal protection of the "free ballot and a fair count" would encourage even Democrats to support black voting rights. Like then-congressman James A. Garfield, Republicans argued that "the constitutional rights of the negro shall be as safe in the hands of one party as it is in the other, and that thus in the south as in the north men may seek their party associates on the great commercial and industrial questions rather than on questions of race and color."

This policy, or gamble, was known as the "New Departure," and its chief architect was President Hayes. As candidate and president, Hayes supported the enforcement of the Reconstruction Amendments, and believed that no real peace between the sections was possible unless the rights of the freedpeople in the South were safeguarded. Hayes was an early supporter of the franchise for African Americans, believing it "sound in principle." In his inaugural address he pledged his support to the "complete protection" of all citizens in the "free enjoyment" of their constitutional rights, and privately he wrote that for the "protection and welfare of the colored people" it was necessary that the three Reconstruction Amendments be "sacredly observed and faithfully enforced." As true as it had been back in

1871, when the Enforcement Acts were passed, the key element in the implementation of the "free ballot and a fair count" policy after 1877 was the Justice Department's enforcement of the Revised Statutes dealing with the franchise.

Hayes's choice for attorney general seemed to auger well for this continued effort. Charles Devens had been a federal marshal in his native Massachusetts before the war, gaining both fame and notoriety in his opposition to the fugitive slave law. After serving as a general in the war, during which he was wounded twice, he became a justice on the Massachusetts state supreme court, the position he held at the time of his appointment as attorney general. From the outset Devens instructed district attorneys, especially in the South, to "vigorously" enforce the federal election statutes. He was well aware of the pitfalls that might be encountered in that effort. He directed federal officials to be as nonpartisan in their actions as possible and to prosecute cases "without inciting more or less political feeling." He also reminded district attorneys to avoid the mistakes made by their predecessors in *Reese* and *Cruikshank*. Writing to Louisiana district attorney A. H. Leonard, Devens pointed out that the "great difficulty" in prosecuting violations of the federal statutes was proving that the "outrage" had been committed on account of the victim's race, color, or previous condition of servitude. He believed that such crimes could be prosecuted "when so many of these occurrences of this nature take place where the parties outraged are always black."

Prosecutions stemming from the 1876 elections and the congressional contests in 1878 were initiated in a number of southern states. The 1878 contests in Louisiana and South Carolina were so marked by fraud and violence that the Senate, which unlike the House remained in Republican hands, created a special investigating committee under the chairmanship of Senator Henry M. Teller of Colorado. Not surprisingly, the Teller Committee's final report catalogued a massive use of fraud and intimidation by Democrats to achieve victory in those two states. In South Carolina just about every county experienced ballot-box stuffing or some type of fraud. The violence and intimidation in Louisiana was reminiscent of 1872. Scores of blacks were reportedly killed or wounded in parishes in the northern part of the state (although Grant Parish was not specifically mentioned), and hundreds driven from their homes by way of intimidation. In one parish the intimidation was so intense that all the Republican candidates simply withdrew from the contest. In New Orleans, "fraud was substituted for violence and very little pains taken to conceal the fact."

Despite the evidence gathered by the Teller Committee and the efforts of Justice Department officials, the prosecutions of election law violations in South Carolina and Louisiana were unsuccessful. The one bright spot was the New Orleans Circuit Court ruling in *In re Goldman* upholding federal jurisdiction, described above. But the problem was not federal authority, it was getting convictions. There was no need for constitutional test cases if the defendants were being set free, and indeed in far too many cases they were not even brought to trial. The reasons for this are not surprising either. The Justice Department's ability to enforce federal law was not much more effective in 1878 than it had been when the Enforcement Acts were first passed eight years earlier. The same problems existed. Department officials met overt and passive resistance at every step of the way. Those accused of violating the law were protected from arrest by their supporters; in some cases entire communities worked to hide the accused or block their seizure, even using armed attacks on U.S. marshals and their deputies. Once arrested, prisoners were often released from custody by their compatriots in well-planned jailbreaks, to disappear again into the protection of a populace hostile to "outside" authority.

But even those arrested and indicted stood a good chance of never being convicted in a court of law. Government witnesses were harassed, intimidated, and worse. Two men on their way to New Orleans to testify in the Louisiana cases in 1878 were taken off a Mississippi River steamboat and killed. Sometimes witnesses disappeared on their own, or simply refused to testify, fearing retribution afterward. (The federal government would not have a witness protection program for almost another century.) And the bureaucratic problems continued. There were constant shortages of funds and manpower despite the overall willingness of Washington to provide these when requested. With no standardized system of accounts or record keeping, local department offices inevitably ran short of funds, and usually at crucial moments in the prosecution of cases.

After 1876 there were two other factors that seriously undermined implementation of the "free ballot" strategy and the protection of black voting rights in the South. Although by 1880 civil service reform had become an important national issue, even more so following President Garfield's assassination, political patronage remained crucial to party loyalty and success. As southern state governments fell under the control of Democrats, the only source of patronage for the Republican Party in the South was federal positions such as postmasters, revenue collectors, and district attorneys and marshals. These appointments became a critical tool in Republican efforts to maintain their southern wing. But this could, and did, result in the appointment of individuals more for their party loyalties than their real abilities to do the job. One notorious example of this was the district attorney in South Carolina, Lucius C. Northrup. A former South Carolina state circuit court judge, Northrup was appointed in August 1877 by President Hayes, over the objections of both national and local party leaders. Northrup's own assistant district attorney, William E. Earle, described him as "incompetent" and his handling of the election cases growing out of the 1878 contest a "blunder from start to end." Despite warnings by the attorney general against politicizing election cases, Northrup did just that. When he failed to get more than a handful of convictions he promptly blamed it on "white democratic" juries. In Northrup's defense it should be noted that he faced a full-scale campaign of resistance against the prosecutions, including the arrest and conviction in state courts of a number of government witnesses on a variety of petty charges. One witness was convicted of perjury in the state court for testimony he had given to the federal grand jury investigating the election cases. He was given a large fine, and in order to pay it so that he could testify at trial Northrup convinced a local Republican leader to mortgage his home.

The growing lack of convictions in election cases after 1878 was also a reflection of another factor, the nature of the crimes themselves. While violence and physical intimidation of African Americans and white Republicans continued unabated through the 1880s, Democrats in the South, perhaps taking a page from their urban counterparts in the North, focused on fraud and deceit to deprive Republican voters of their influence and to maintain their own hold on political power. The variety of the types of fraud used was impressive. Ballots and ballot boxes were regularly lost, stolen, or tampered with in some fashion, especially in voting districts with significant numbers of Republican voters. Democrats also made use of fraudulent ballots. Since each party was responsible for printing up their own ballots with their ticket of candidates, Democrats contrived to make theirs appear to be Republican ballots. One common, and especially devious, way to do this was to print ballots with a portrait on top of Abraham Lincoln. The idea behind this was, of course, that large numbers of southern black voters, being illiterate, would recognize the face of the "Great Emancipator," and therefore believe they were casting a Republican vote when in reality they were voting for the Democratic candidates!

By far the most common fraud used was ballot-box stuffing. In one South Carolina district in 1878, the final Democratic vote count was 3,500. Not only was this figure higher than the total number of registered voters in the district, it also meant that someone had voted every thirteen seconds continuously throughout the day. But how could this happen? The answer in South Carolina, and in other states as well, was the use of the so-called "tissue-ballot," or "kiss-ballot" as it was more commonly called. Basically, the "kiss-ballot" looked like a single Democratic ballot, but in fact it was a number, usually three to five, of very thin, identical ballots stuck loosely together at the corners. After the polls closed it was necessary for someone to shake or mishandle the ballot box (hence, the "kiss") in order to separate the ballots. One hundred Democratic votes suddenly became five hundred! In an attempt to combat this type of fraud, federal election supervisors, when present, had the authority to make sure the number of ballots counted at the end of election day did not exceed the number of registered voters on the polling lists in that district. When it did, they were blindfolded and withdrew from the box only the number of possible votes. Even this proved ineffective since the large number of tissue-ballots usually guaranteed a Democratic majority anyway.

Northrup, for one, was confident that cases involving this type of fraud would be successful. "The law," he declared, "seemed to be made for the tissue ballots and tissue ballots for the law." In reality, the opposite appeared to be true. Convictions for this and many other types of fraud were extremely difficult to prove after the fact. The whole idea behind the use of fraud was secrecy, including making sure there were as few witnesses as possible. And what was witnessed, a Democratic Party worker "accidentally" dropping the ballot box, was difficult to prove criminal. And since such methods inevitably resulted in Democratic victories, it was difficult for district attorneys to convince juries that these cases were not partisan or a form of legal sour grapes. And Democrats were only too happy to point out, although no federal cases were ever prosecuted, that Republicans used the same tactics.

Republicans' New Departure policies for revitalizing the party in the South through the protection of the "free ballot and a fair count" continued under Presidents Garfield, Arthur, and Harrison. While the specific political calculus behind this strategy varied with the different administrations, all centered on the protection of the elective franchise. All three presidents at some point expressed their strong support for the continued protection of civil and political rights of blacks in the South, a support manifest in their appointment of attorneys general who shared this commitment. Between 1880 and 1894 Justice Department officials brought hundreds of election cases in the South, and their admitted lack of convictions should not obscure the substantial effort made. As President William H. Harrison noted in 1889, "The freedom of the ballot is a condition of national life, and no power vested in Congress or in the Executive to secure and perpetuate it should remain unused."

CHAPTER 8

"That Evil Was Possible"

Up until the 1950s historians and other scholars generally accepted the notion that the disfranchisement of African-American voters was both the immediate and the inevitable result of the Supreme Court's rulings in *Reese* and *Cruikshank*. This was not especially remarkable since disfranchisement mirrored the equally swift denial after 1877 of nearly all social and civil rights of blacks in the South and the imposition of legally sanctioned racial segregation. However, in 1955, the historian C. Vann Woodward published *The Strange Career of Jim Crow*, based on a series of lectures he had given at the University of Virginia. Woodward argued that "Jim Crow" segregation did not appear full-blown throughout the South immediately after 1877. Race relations during the last quarter of the nineteenth century were in fact characterized by their "variety and inconsistency," not only from state to state, but within each state as well. African Americans sometimes blocked, or at least postponed, attempts to segregate them. They often used tactics, such as a streetcar boycott in Louisville, Kentucky, in the early 1870s, that presaged strategies employed during the civil rights movement in the next century.

However strange Jim Crow's career may have been, it was aided by a series of Supreme Court rulings in the late nineteenth century that fatally undermined national protection of blacks' social and civil rights. Through its interpretation of the Thirteenth and Fourteenth Amendments the Court virtually eliminated federal protection of such rights. At the same time it allowed states nearly unfettered authority to impose racial discrimination. The two major pieces of federal civil rights legislation passed during Reconstruction, the Civil Rights Acts of 1866 and 1875, had been rarely enforced by Justice Department officials in the South. But both measures provided the Court in the late nineteenth century with the opportunity to redefine the meaning of the first two Reconstruction Amendments. The process began in 1873. That year the Supreme Court provided its first important interpretation of the Fourteenth Amendment in the *Slaughterhouse Cases*. Significantly, the case did not even involve those whom the amendment was intended to protect. A group of white New Orleans butchers argued that a state law requiring them to use a specific slaughterhouse violated their rights under the Fourteenth Amendment. They maintained that their right to engage in business was one of those "privileges and immunities" protected from state interference by the Fourteenth Amendment. In upholding the state regulation, the Supreme Court majority narrowly confined federally protected rights to such things as the right to travel to the nation's capital, the right to habeas corpus, and the right to use the nation's ports and navigable rivers. By implication, all other rights, including those most relevant to daily lives of the freedpeople, were left to the states to protect, or not. That same year, in *Bradwell v. Illinois*, the Supreme Court again narrowly defined those civil rights that fell under federal protection. In another case that did not involve African Americans, the Court rejected a white Illinois woman's attempt to use the Fourteenth Amendment to overturn that state's refusal to admit her to the practice of law. By again narrowly defining what rights fell under federal protection, the Court further expanded the range of rights still under state authority.

The next step came in 1883. In the *Civil Rights Cases* the Supreme Court narrowed the range of federal civil rights protection even more directly when it struck down key sections of the Civil Rights Act of 1875. That measure forbade racial discrimination in places of public accommodation such as restaurants, hotels, public conveyances, and theaters. Citing the Court's earlier ruling in *Cruikshank*, Justice Bradley's majority opinion accepted the "state action doctrine" used by the defense attorneys in the Louisiana case. Under this doctrine federal protections guaranteed by all three Reconstruction amendments applied only to cases of formal action by the state, in the form of a law or statute, or by official representatives of the state acting for or on behalf of the state. The Fourteenth Amendment, Justice Bradley announced, "does not authorize Congress to create a code of municipal law for the regulation of private rights; but to provide modes of redress against the operation of State laws, and the action of State officers, executive or judicial, when these are subversive of the fundamental rights specified in the amendment." This narrow view of the Fourteenth Amendment's reach clearly reflected Bradley's earlier circuit court opinion in *Cruikshank*.

The *Civil Rights Cases* also revealed a new, and lone, dissenting voice. Appointed to the Supreme Court by President Hayes in 1877, Kentuckian John Marshall Harlan was a former slaveholder who became a committed Republican during Reconstruction. It will be recalled that he assisted the federal district attorney in arguing the *Reese* case in Kentucky. Justice Harlan's dissenting opinion in the *Civil Rights Cases* was as passionate and indignant as Justice Hunt's dissent had been eight years earlier in *Reese*. Hunt, however, had resigned from the Court in 1882. Like Hunt, Harlan accused the majority of a "narrow and artificial" reading of the Reconstruction Amendments that used arbitrary distinctions and legal niceties to subvert the true meaning and intent of those measures. For Harlan nothing was more certain than that these amendments were intended to protect the rights of former slaves as "freemen and citizens" and that Congress had the clear authority to pass laws that would bring this about. He argued that the social discrimination prohibited in the federal statute was nothing less than a "badge of servitude" that Congress had the authority to eliminate. Harlan reserved his most righteous scorn for Bradley's hypocritical contention that the freedpeople in the South had reached the point, through the aid of "beneficent legislation," where they should now be considered as "mere" citizens and no longer the "special favorite of the laws." Harlan rightly saw this as an admission not only that Reconstruction was truly over, but that southern states were now being given a wide degree of latitude when it came to determining the form and substance of acceptable "social discrimination."

With the Court's ruling in the *Civil Rights Cases*, southern state legislatures, as well as local governments, took the opportunity to turn "mere" racial discrimination into law. The means was a series of "Jim Crow" statutes and regulations that essentially set up a system of racial separation in almost all aspects of daily life. (In South Africa in the 1940s this system, with the ominous designation "apartheid," would be used to subjugate the majority black population.) In 1896 the Supreme Court signaled its constitutional approval of segregation in *Plessy v. Ferguson*, by upholding a Louisiana law requiring separate railroad cars for blacks and whites. The Court's majority opinion, written by Republican justice Henry B. Brown, decided that the law did not violate the Fourteenth Amendment so long as the separate facilities provided each race were "equal." Brown rejected the notion that such "enforced separation" was state discrimination because it "stamps the colored race with a badge of inferiority." He noted that if this was the case it was not the intent of the law itself, but "solely because the colored race chooses to put that construction upon it." The Fourteenth Amendment was intended to "enforce absolute equality between the races before the law," but it could not do away with "distinctions" based on race or "enforce . . . a commingling of the two races upon terms unsatisfactory to either." Justice Harlan was again a lone dissenter, and made many of the same arguments he had voiced earlier in the *Civil Rights Cases*. For Harlan, the Court's defense of racial segregation was just a "thin disguise" for the very kind of racial "discrimination" they had earlier said was beyond the power of the federal government to prohibit. The purpose of the Fourteenth Amendment was to ensure that the states could not make the class distinctions based on race that the majority was now accepting. "Our Constitution," Harlan proclaimed, "is color-blind and neither knows nor tolerates classes among its citizens."

Over the next decade southern states put laws into place that extended racial separation to almost every aspect of daily social and economic life, from public transportation to dining and recreation, and to every stage of life, from hospitals to schools to cemeteries. What made an injustice a tragedy was, as Harlan himself predicted, that southern states showed no intention of ensuring that the "equal" part of the "separate but equal" doctrine was carried out. African Americans could expect to be born, to live, to be hospitalized, educated, entertained, and buried in separate and decidedly inferior facilities and institutions

If, as C. Vann Woodward claimed, segregation did not appear immediately and throughout the South after 1877, neither did disfranchisement. Indeed, Woodward admitted that one of the factors hindering the spread of segregation was the substantial numbers of blacks who continued to vote in the South after 1877. Republican leaders continued to believe that the party had a future there and that the protection of the "free ballot and a fair count" might preserve this future. In addition, Republicans attempted to take advantage of the growing economic discontent in the South, especially among farmers, by seeking alliance with so-called Independent movements that sprang up in a number of southern states in the last two decades of the century. Primarily dissident Democrats, these parties went by a variety of names that reflected their particular concerns. In Virginia, for example, the Readjusters broke with Democrats over the issue of scaling back the state debt. Led by former Confederate general William Mahone, the Readjusters openly, and successfully, courted the black vote in the early 1880s. In Texas and Louisiana the Democratic insurgency took the form of the Greenback Party. Its platform called for monetary inflation, through the increased circulation of paper currency, in order to aid rural debtors. During the 1890s the Populist or People's Party provided the primary threat to Democratic hegemony in the South. What these parties and movements shared with Republicans was a common need for the protection of honest and fair election. As a result they generally supported federal franchise enforcement as a way to attract African-American votes.

Yet even as the courts were upholding federal authority over the electoral process, support for such protection began to wane. A number of factors accounted for this. Politically, the New Departure attempts to revive southern Republicanism proved increasingly futile. In addition, Independent leaders and their parties often turned out to be as hostile to African-American social and political rights as the Democrats. This was certainly the case with the Populists. Some of the most prominent southern Populists leaders, like Georgia's Tom Watson, began as advocates for racial political alliance and ended up rabid segregationists. In addition, the Democratic Party became stronger nationally. Democrat Grover Cleveland captured the presidency in 1884, and again in 1892. By the 1880s Americans generally were becoming less interested in the "Southern question" and more concerned with economic issues arising out of industrialization.

An important consequence of these factors was that even those Republicans who had once been among the strongest proponents of franchise rights were now willing to discuss the wisdom of having extended voting rights to African Americans in the first place. In the spring of 1879 a forum devoted to the question "Ought the Negro to Be Disfranchised? Ought He to Have Been Enfranchised?" appeared in the respected journal *The North American Review*. The seven contributors to the forum constituted a who's who of political leaders of both parties. Maine senator and Republican presidential aspirant James G. Blaine presented both the opening and closing articles, and between were pieces by soon-to-be president James A. Garfield, abolitionist icon Wendell Phillips, Democratic vice-presidential candidate Thomas Hendricks, southern Democratic Senator Wade Hampton, former Confederate vice president Alexander Stephens, future Democratic Supreme Court justice L. Q. C. Lamar, and southern Democrat firebrand Montgomery Blair. All were white, and with the exception of Blair, all more or less agreed that the answer to the first question was no, and the answer to the second, yes. What made the collection of articles significant was not the answers as such, but the fact that only nine years after ratification of the Fifteenth Amendment, these questions were being asked at all. Blaine pointedly denied that it was the result of "any cooling of philanthropic interest" in the fate of southern blacks or any "radical or novel" view about universal suffrage. Rather, the questions were asked because "in the judgement of many of those hitherto accounted wisest, negro suffrage has failed to attain the ends hoped for when the franchise was conferred." In other words, the Fifteenth Amendment was not simply the extension of a particular right to a group of free, and supposedly equal, citizens, but it had also been a kind of test for the freedpeople, and now the "wisest" were to decide if they had passed.

In judging African Americans' performance at the ballot box, the contributors developed two related themes. First, almost all the participants agreed that granting the franchise had not been a mistake. However, the lack of education had proven a critical stumbling block in allowing an "ignorant" and "un-educated" people to successfully exercise their rights. By this time northern philanthropists, Protestant missionaries, and Republicans of the postabolitionist tradition had already begun efforts to create a network of schools and colleges for African Americans across the South. The goal of the freedpeople was not more rights, but more education. With education (even if segregated), they could then demonstrate their worthiness to enjoy the rights of citizenship. Southern contributors Montgomery Blair and Alexander Stephens sounded the second theme, one not directly challenged by the most ardent supporters of black franchise rights, such as Phillips and Garfield. This theme centered on the failure of congressional Reconstruction, and by 1889 the theme was gaining increasing popularity in the South. Reconstruction had failed because the national government had attempted to literally revolutionize the South by "imposing" draconian restrictions on white southerners, legislating equality, and giving political power to those who had never exercised it before. The "instrument" of this continued northern oppression was black enfranchisement. Republicans in Congress, and their southern henchmen, the carpetbaggers, had manipulated and used black voters and officeholders for their own selfish purposes. The result, wrote Blair, was "the most disgraceful chapter in our history." Republican regimes in the South during Reconstruction were cesspools of corruption and incompetence that ended only when Democrats successfully "redeemed" their states and restored honest and genuine government to the people.

Blair's underlying rationale for Reconstruction's failure was not merely a tyrannical national government. It was also based on racism. Bolstered by the growing influence of social Darwinian theories of differential racial development, southerners, and growing numbers of northerners, more openly rejected the very idea of any sort of racial equality. According to Blair, black people came from the "tropics," where "despotism has prevailed for all ages." Expecting them to be able to govern themselves, let alone vote for others, was as "reasonable" as expecting them "to develop wings by training." Nor was Blair alone. John T. Morgan, senator from Alabama from 1877 to 1907, regularly defended the premise that the two races never were and never could be equal. Morgan proudly insisted that, despite the natural state of conflict existing between the races, relations between blacks and whites in the South were more "friendly" than in the North. They were based on the recognition "by both races, of the leadership and superiority of the white race." He was especially open about the deepest fear of growing numbers of southerners, race amalgamation. The inevitable result of intermarriage would be the destruction of the white race. "One drop of Negro blood known to exist in the veins of a woman," Morgan wrote, "draws her down to the social status of a Negro."

Not surprisingly, Morgan believed that any attempt to make African Americans equal—especially politically—was a mistake and doomed to failure. In a February 1889 magazine article entitled "Shall Negro Majorities Rule," Morgan argued that "we have not accomplished any good to either race by conferring upon 1,500,000 Negroes the privilege of voting." The Fifteenth Amendment was a mistake, since it served to incite former slaves "to persistent effort to accomplish the impossible result of race equality." All the laws, federal or otherwise, intended to protect this right of the "inferior Negro race," even by force, would fail because they were opposed by the vast majority of the "white race." Indeed, Morgan warned against any "outside pressure" or attempts to deny the South complete control over the fate of black voters, threatening that any such "agitation" could only cause blacks more pain and suffering since it would foster the false illusion that African Americans could ever be equal.

In spite of the attitudes exemplified by the *Review*'s contributors, and the Supreme Court's unsympathetic rulings on race since the *Slaughterhouse Cases*, not all northern Republicans were willing to completely abandon the cause of African-American voters in the South. In 1890 Senator George Frisbie Hoar and Representative Henry Cabot Lodge, both Massachusetts Republicans, introduced a new election bill in Congress. The Federal Election Law, or Lodge Bill as it came to be called, was essentially an updated version of the earlier election statutes and was primarily intended "for the more efficient enforcement of such laws." It reaffirmed and clarified the role of federal election supervisors and federal courts over the electoral process in congressional contests, following closely the assertion of national authority set out by the Supreme Court in its earlier rulings in *Yarbrough* and *Siebold*. Although Republican managers of the measure recognized its particular applicability to the protection of African-American voters in the South, the language and reach of the act were in keeping with the "free ballot and fair count" strategy of Republicans in the 1880s to combat electoral fraud and corruption in all parts of the country. The most significant innovation in the measure was the creation of a United States Board of Canvassers. In any congressional district in which irregularities involving fraud, bribery, or intimidation were alleged to have occurred, the federal circuit court judge for that district could appoint, on a nonpartisan basis, three persons from the community to examine the election returns and the allegations brought. These three were then authorized to "certify" the winner, that is, the House candidate-elect (Congress still having its constitutional authority to seat or not seat its own members). Those accused of wrongdoing were subject to indictment and punishments in federal courts.

With a solid Republican majority in the House, the bill passed easily in that chamber in July of 1890. But when Senator Hoar introduced the measure in the Senate it ran into a firestorm of opposition, not only from Democrats but from a number of Republican senators more concerned with passing tariff and monetary legislation. Democrats dubbed the measure the "Force Bill."

By constantly repeating this label they raised the specter of federal troops once again occupying and terrorizing helpless southern states and citizens as they had done during Reconstruction. In fact, there was no mention of the use of troops or even U.S. marshals in the bill. (Although, in fairness to the Democrats, the provisions for the use of federal forces in cases of insurrection and civil unrest remained part of the Revised Statutes. Ironically, the use of federal troops in this type of situation would first be authorized by Democratic president Grover Cleveland against the striking workers of the Pullman Railroad Car Company in Chicago in 1894.) Indeed, Democratic senators dragged out just about every argument against voting rights and federal authority made since the beginning of Reconstruction. Now added to their arsenal were openly expressed sentiments of racial superiority; rejection of the Fifteenth Amendment as a "blunder" and an "indefensible political crime"; and accusations that the bill was nothing more than an attempt to revive sectional division and old enmities.

Senate Democrats were able to postpone consideration of the bill until after the November 1890 elections. Hoar went along with this after obtaining a signed written pledge by all but one of his fellow Republicans to support the measure. When the bill did come up again in January 1891, Democrats once more launched a series of attacks and maneuvers to defeat the measure. They succeeded, but only because several of the so-called Silver Republicans ignored their earlier commitment. On January 26, 1891, by a vote of thirty-five to thirty-four, the Lodge Bill was formally set aside from any further consideration. Hoar was furious. He accused fellow Republicans who had voted with the majority of breaking the "pledge" that the Republican Party had made to the freedpeople during Reconstruction and ever since. He saved his most passionate reproach for Democrats, who he claimed, had "honored" him with their abuse during his management of the bill. In particular he castigated southern senators for their hypocrisy in proclaiming their commitment to and record of "free and fair elections" in their states. Cataloguing the many documented instances of political fraud and intimidation, he prophesied that relations between the races in the South could be one of freedom, honor, peace, and prosperity if only southerners spent "one tenth of the energy" they expended in denying blacks any opportunity to improve or exercise their constitutional rights. "You have tried everything else," Hoar concluded, "try justice."

Unfortunately, by that time the South's political agenda did not include justice, at least as it was understood by Hoar and those who supported the election law. Nor was it still high on the nation's list of priorities. While the Lodge Bill's passage in the House and close Senate vote can be seen as evidence of the continued commitment of Republicans to the protection of the "free ballot and a fair count" and the cause of African-American franchise rights, it also marked the very real end to the federal government's role in implementing those policies for more than another half century. During the 1892 elections Justice Department officials in the South brought only a handful of prosecutions under the statutes. Most were unsuccessful, and a year later Congress repealed almost all sections of the Revised Statutes dealing with federal election law enforcement. The repeal debate was much shorter, but just as bitter as the Lodge Bill, and the final vote was again due to the defection of Silver Republicans. The point had been made. Senator John C. Spooner, one of the Lodge Bill's most ardent supporters and an opponent of repeal, admitted as much. He concluded that "the interest of the Republicans of the United States in an honest ballot, in maintaining the rights of citizenship, and in holding sacred the pledge of Abraham Lincoln's proclamation to the colored man is dead, or in a slumber too deep for us to arouse it."

Although symbolic of the national government's intent no longer to protect the black vote, the defeat of the Lodge Bill, and the subsequent repeal of the election statutes, did not disfranchise a single black voter. But southern intentions in that regard were made abundantly clear during the debates over the bills. Both sides made repeated reference to the so-called Mississippi Plan. The term itself originally appeared in the 1870s as a blueprint for using violence to overthrow the Republican regime in the state, a plan quickly followed by other southern states. Following the end of Reconstruction, the term reflected less a strategy of capturing political power than of holding on to it by disfranchising black voters. In 1890, just prior to the introduction of the Lodge Bill in Congress, Mississippians held a convention to draft a new state constitution. Several provisions in the new state constitution, including those establishing a literacy requirement and a poll tax, altered the qualifications for voting. Presented as "reform" measures, the provisions were obviously intended to eliminate as many African-American voters as possible. The problem, of course, was to do so without violating the Fourteenth and Fifteenth Amendments, or disqualifying large numbers of whites. As one convention delegate bluntly put it, "To avoid the disfranchisement of a lot of white ignoramuses we can't have an educational qualification, and to pander to the prejudices of those who have no property we cannot have a property qualification."

The problem was solved by skillful wording of the provisions that allowed for official discretion in implementing the qualifications. In the case of the literacy requirement, every potential voter had to be able to read any section of the state constitution or "be able to understand the same when read to him, or give a reasonable interpretation thereof." That left it entirely up to state registrars to determine the level of "understanding" of any and all applicants. It was understood "that any white illiterate would be passed," while no African American would. In the case of the poll tax, there were sufficient qualifications of this requirement to ensure its unequal implementation. In addition to meeting age and residency requirements, applicants could have their payment refused if they had a criminal record. Not surprisingly, there was even a specified list of crimes applicable, which included offenses, such as public drunkenness, theft, and vagrancy, for which blacks were most often prosecuted. But the most devious catch was that a prospective voter could not pay the poll tax unless he "could read and comprehend the Constitution" first. To ensure continued disfranchisement of those rejected, a person could not pay the tax if he had not paid for the two preceding years.

Individually, these elements of what came to be called the Mississippi Plan were not new. The poll tax, for example, had been used before, and the refusal to accept payment of this type of tax in Lexington, Kentucky, in 1872 had resulted in the *Reese* case. The Mississippi Plan became the blueprint for disfranchisement of black voters elsewhere in the South after 1890 because it embodied a "cocktail" approach to removing African Americans from the polling lists. Almost all the southern states would adopt two or more complementary methods to accomplish disfranchisement. They did so by following Mississippi's method of revising their state constitutions. By making these restrictions part of their fundamental state charters, southerners argued that the restrictions represented the true will of the people of the state, rather than the possibly spurious actions of a particular state legislative majority. Southern whites also defended the use of both state constitution revision and legislative action as their own response to the problem of electoral reform. Such initiatives, they argued, were necessary to ensure honest and open elections. Although unwittingly or not, they were at the same time admitting that the earlier fraud and intimidation hadn't been effective enough in eliminating the political threat to white Democratic supremacy.

Between 1890 and 1905 most of the states of the former Confederacy revised their state constitutions in special conventions to include provisions aimed at the disfranchisement of African-American voters. The other states, as well as border states like Maryland, West Virginia, and Kentucky, did so by constitutional amendments or legislative action. The most common method for suffrage restriction was the poll tax, usually in combination with one or more methods such as the literacy test. Those states with literacy tests usually included a Mississippi-style "understanding clause" as well. Other methods were also introduced to achieve the same result. In South and North Carolina poll taxes and literacy tests supplemented the use of multiple ballot boxes. On election day voters were faced with six to eight different ballot boxes, one each for various local, state, and federal offices to be contested. South Carolina had implemented the "Eight Box Law" as early as 1882. In one sense the law was a form of literacy test, since it required voters to deposit their ballot in the correctly labeled box. Ballots placed in the wrong box were automatically discarded. It also gave election managers the opportunity to enable illiterates to vote "right" by advising them where to put their ballots "and let others void their ballots through ignorance." Prior to the repeal of the federal election statutes in 1893, the use of multiple ballot boxes also hampered Justice Department enforcement of the federal election laws. State officials claimed jurisdiction over the boxes used for local and state offices, and did everything they could to control these boxes before, during, and particularly after election day.

Supplementing these laws were a variety of formal and informal practices intended to restrict and eliminate the black vote. Whereas earlier opposition to the exercise of franchise rights had focused on voting and the election-day part of the process, after 1890 southern states focused on the voter registration process. As with the methods employed above, the primary goals were to allow state officials as much discretion as possible to interpret and to implement any of the prerequisites or requirements for voting. The goal was to make it as difficult as possible for even those African Americans qualified to vote to register. Times and places for voter registration were changed with bewildering frequency, or scheduled for times and at places that required an extraordinary commitment on the part of a potential voter to even attempt to register. For example, in rural areas voters were often required to register during specified periods. These periods always seem to coincide with the busiest times of spring planting and fall harvesting seasons. Of course, registration offices were open only during the workday, and if the offices were located in town courthouses or city halls, this virtually guaranteed loss of an entire day's salary or fieldwork for registrants traveling from outlying areas by foot or mule.

State officials responsible for registering voters were given wide latitude to interpret and enforce the various qualifications. Even for standard prerequisites that required specific information, such as age and residency, registration officials could determine the kind and amount of evidence needed by a potential registrant to qualify. African-American men born as slaves often did not know their date of birth, let alone were they able to produce some formal documentation if asked. Since home and land ownership remained closed to most blacks in the South, the absence of tangible proof of residency could also be used as a reason to refuse registration on the poll lists. And then there were the exemptions. Sometimes built into the laws, sometimes simply assumed by officials on their own, ways were devised to enable officials to let whites register, while the applications of equally qualified, or equally unqualified, blacks were rejected. The most infamous example of this was the "grandfather clause." The clause was often misinterpreted as a disqualifying device aimed at potential black voters, that is, if your grandfather couldn't vote, neither could you. In fact, the clause was an exemption for white registrants who might otherwise not meet the prerequisites, that is, if your grandfather served in the Confederate army you didn't have to pass the literacy test. In some states registrars could also pass on the good "moral character" of a potential voter, which of course left it up to individual registrars to determine what constituted either the standard for making such a judgment or the necessary evidence to prove it. Given these real and potential barriers, as time passed many otherwise qualified African-American voters simply chose not to even attempt to register to vote rather than face the ordeals they knew awaited them.

Despite the emphasis on the registration process to restrict black voting, southerners did not ignore elections themselves as an opportunity to further disfranchisement. In the wake of the *Yarbrough* decision and other Supreme Court rulings that upheld national authority over elections for federal officials, southern states changed the dates of elections for state and local offices, most often to the odd years between congressional contests. This was obviously intended to restrict possible federal interference to the congressional and presidential contests. It also tended to discouraged voter turnout. As the South became progressively "solid" Democratic, this had a greater adverse impact on opposition parties and their potential supporters. Indeed, the emergence of the Solid South encouraged Democrats to adopt another form of election, the "white primary." During the Progressive reform period between 1900 and the end of World War I, the primary election, in which party candidates sought nomination through special elections, was widely promoted and adopted in many states. Supporters of the primary election believed it would help cleanse American politics of the unhealthy influence of the special interests and party bosses and result in the selection of better officeholders. In the South Democrats welcomed the primary as a way to keep dissent and conflict within the party. Because it was designed as a party mechanism apart from the government, party officials could be even more openly restrictive in who could participate in these nominating contests. By the 1920s the Democratic primary had become the real election in many parts of the South. Generally, the winner of the Democratic primary contest faced no, or only token, opposition in the general election.

The use of the secret or "Australian" ballot spread nationally after 1890. Advocates presented the secret ballot as an electoral reform that would help clean up politics and make voters more independent of outside economic or political pressures. In the South, where previously party-produced ballots had made it easy to vote the entire party "ticket," the secret ballot proved an effective disfranchising tool. It often provided voters with a second literacy test. The single secret ballot now listed candidates by office rather than party. Voters now had to have the ability to read and correctly identify the name or party affiliation. While theoretically voters could not have anyone in the polling booth with them, there always seemed to be a Democratic Party worker around to "help" a confused voter.

In 1875 the Supreme Court had affirmed in both *Reese* and *Cruikshank* that, whatever else it encompassed, the Fifteenth Amendment did prohibit states from denying the right to vote on the basis of race. Were these various state restrictions, especially literacy tests and poll taxes, a violation of that Amendment, and if so, wouldn't the Court find them unconstitutional? By the last years of the nineteenth century the Supreme Court itself had undergone an almost complete turnover of personnel. Three of the new justices, including Chief Justice Melville W. Fuller in 1888, were appointees of Democratic president Grover Cleveland. But even those justices appointed by Republican presidents Arthur and Harrison reflected differing attitudes from their predecessors. These "new conservative" justices, Democrat and Republican, were both more suspicious of national authority and far more interested in protecting the property rights of business corporations than in protecting the political and civil rights of citizens of whatever race. Indeed, it was the Fuller Court that accepted the doctrine that the due process clause of the Fifth and Fourteenth Amendments provided substantive limits on state and federal economic regulation. Business corporations overshadowed African Americans as "persons" to be protected from government infringement of their rights. Moreover, the racial views of even those new justices who were both northern and Republican were closer to racist sentiments expressed earlier in the *North American Review.*

In this context the Supreme Court's response to state disfranchisement efforts after 1890 was not unexpected. In 1897 in the case *Williams v. Mississippi*, the Court ruled that state voter restrictions were permissible. Remarkably, although the Mississippi constitution of 1890 was at issue in the case, the Fifteenth Amendment was not even mentioned. The Court in *Williams* was asked to decide whether the way in which juries in the state were empaneled violated the equal protection clause of the Fourteenth Amendment. The case involved an African-American defendant, Henry Williams, who had been indicted for murder by an all-white grand jury in a state court. He claimed that since juries were taken from voter registration lists, the suffrage restrictions of the 1890 constitution inevitably resulted in all-white panels. In 1880 the Supreme Court, in *Strauder v. West Virginia*, had in fact ruled that a West Virginia law excluding blacks from juries was unconstitutional. Now in 1897 a unanimous Court ignored both this earlier precedent and the Fifteenth Amendment and ruled that neither Mississippi's constitutional provisions nor their "administration" was discriminatory. There was, the Court said, "an allegation of the purpose of the convention to disfranchise citizens of the colored race, but of this we have no concern." The

Supreme Court acknowledged that state laws that denied persons "equal justice" or that were applied and administered "with an evil eye and an unequal hand" were prohibited. But the Mississippi constitution did no such thing. Literacy tests and poll taxes were not "on their face" discriminatory, and in the Court's view their administration was "not evil." The only thing the justices were willing to recognize was "that evil was possible under them."

The Supreme Court's refusal in *Williams* to recognize the possibility of the "evil" intent behind the Mississippi Plan did for voting rights what *Plessy* did for racial segregation. It completed the process of judicial abandonment begun back in 1875 in *Reese* and *Cruikshank* by approving almost complete state authority over the electoral process. One by one southern states adopted their own Mississippi Plans. The cumulative impact of these various state restrictions and stratagems was irresistible. Although exact percentages are subject to interpretation, it is certain that by the early years of the twentieth century the vast majority of African Americans in the South had lost their right to vote. Over the next two decades that percentage increased steadily, and it is fair to say that by the 1930s almost all African Americans in the South (including women after 1919) could not vote.

And what about Louisiana and Kentucky, where the two cases in this story began? Despite the massacre, Republicans maintained a precarious control in Grant Parish, Louisiana, for another few years, but violence there and elsewhere in the state continued, reaching a peak in the summer of 1874. Following Justice Bradley's circuit court ruling overturning the indictments, the defendants were treated to a "hero's welcome" in the parish. That resulted in more mayhem and another unprovoked and unpunished murder of a black man. Gradually, such overt violence and terror abated. White Democrats turned to a strategy based on appeals to racial solidarity, white supremacy, and fear of renewed federal intervention to both discredit and court moderate whites. It worked. By 1876 Democrats controlled both state and parish governments. Yet in 1879 Louisiana Democrats were still not politically entrenched enough to put suffrage restrictions into their new state constitution, and for most of the next several decades they resorted to the use of fraud to maintain and solidify their hold on power. In 1898 another constitutional convention displayed no such hesitation. A series of permanent disfranchising provisions was enacted that included a literacy test, property qualifications, an eventual poll tax, and a grandfather-clause exemption for whites.

Kentucky's status as a slave state not a part of the Confederacy, as seen previously, made it both similar to and different than the rest of the South in both its Reconstruction and late-nineteenth-century development in terms of race relations and civil rights. After 1877, blacks in Kentucky endured a continuing campaign of lynching and mob violence. While Jim Crow segregation was eventually imposed, the state did not institute formal disfranchisement. Part of the reason for this was the continued presence of the Republican Party in the state. Even after 1895 Republican governors, as well as other state and local officials, continued to be elected. There were occasional, but unsuccessful, efforts to introduce suffrage requirements. Democrats tried first attracting African-American voters to the party and then completely ignoring them. When they felt it necessary, Democrats were as willing as their counterparts farther south to resort to blatant appeals for racial solidarity. In one instance after 1900, women in Lexington were given the right to vote in local school elections, only to see that right taken away amid fears of a larger turnout among black women. Republicans proved equally unsupportive by continuing, as they had during Reconstruction, to exclude blacks from patronage consideration and from selection as candidates for office, especially in urban areas with significant numbers of black voters. In addition, black voters continued to fall victim to the same kinds of informal barriers they experienced in the early 1870s through voter registration and election day fraud. Kentucky blacks found that political marginalization in a segregated society was not much different from disfranchisement.

And what of Hiram Reese, Mathew Fouchee, William Cruikshank, and the other defendants involved in the two cases? Despite the enthusiasm with which they were welcomed home,

Cruikshank and the other Louisiana defendants all seem to have disappeared immediately into that personal historical obscurity especially reserved for one or both parties in a Supreme Court decision. The historical record is equally silent on Hiram Reese and his fellow inspectors. What they, and others like them, represented during this period is a different matter. In 1879, a North Carolina carpetbagger by the name of Albion W. Tourgee published a novel entitled *A Fool's Errand*. As a writer, publicist, and lawyer, Tourgee would become one of the most consistent and outspoken white champions of African-American rights in the late nineteenth century. The high point of his career was his involvement as one of the attorneys fighting the Louisiana railroad segregation law in the *Plessy* case. His novel was a partially autobiographical account of a former Union army officer's sojourn in the South during the Reconstruction years. Although written almost two decades before the actual fact, Tourgee's description of what the officer, the "Fool," discovered about his adoptive home provides a fitting epitaph for the story that began with Cruikshank's role in the Grant Parish massacre and Hiram Reese's denial of William Garner's vote:

The revolution had been inaugurated, and its feasibility demonstrated. Henceforth, it was only a question of time as to its absolute and universal success. The rule of the majority had been overthrown, the power of the Government boldly defied, and its penalties for crime successfully evaded, that the enfranchisement of the colored man might be rendered a farce; and the obnoxious Amendments and Reconstruction legislation had been shown to be practically nullified. Read by the light of other days, the triumph of the ancient South was incredibly grand; in the then present there was little lacking to give it completeness; in the future—well, that could take care of itself.

Conclusion

The ending of one story of the past often discloses the beginning of another. By the end of the nineteenth century it was clear that the federal government and the Republican Party had failed to make good on their implicit pledge to the freedpeople with the Fifteenth Amendment and the enforcement legislation during and after Reconstruction. This failure, combined with the legal disfranchisement of African-American voters in the South after 1890, marked the closure of an important chapter in the history of African Americans and voting rights. Yet even as the number of black voters in the South dwindled to minuscule proportions, the campaign began to restore the franchise and make good on that original pledge. Even as the era of Jim Crow segregation and disfranchisement was under way, the seeds of black protest were being sown. African-American leaders and organizations were not about to let the future "take care of itself."

During the early years of the twentieth century African Americans created a number of national organizations to protest their unequal status, sometimes with the support of sympathetic northern whites. Groups like the Afro-American League, the Negro Fellowship League, and the New England Suffrage League sought ways to combat segregation and restore voting rights. The most prominent such organization was the National Association for the Advancement of Colored People, founded in New York in 1909 by black leaders such as W. E. B. DuBois and Ida Wells-Barnett, along with a number of prominent white liberals. From its beginning the NAACP had as its priority the protection of equal rights and an end to segregation and disfranchisement. The Tenth Annual Report of the organization in 1919 listed as its first goal "A vote for every Negro man and woman on the same terms as for white men and women." To achieve its aims the NAACP concentrated its resources on legislatures and courtrooms. While early on the legislative focus was on passage of antilynching laws, the organization immediately began court challenges to suffrage restrictions. In 1915 the NAACP won its first victory when it convinced the U.S. Supreme Court to declare the Oklahoma grandfather clause unconstitutional. In *Guinn v. Oklahoma* a unanimous Court ruled that since the exemption was based on a date prior to the Fifteenth Amendment, it was clearly intended to exclude blacks. Therefore, it was "in direct and positive disregard of the Fifteenth Amendment." This sort of restriction, the Court agreed, created the very "conditions which the Amendment was intended to destroy." In fact, by this time the grandfather clause had already become less effective as the Civil War generation died off and the number of eligible white southerners sharply declined. Nonetheless, a year after *Guinn* Oklahoma passed a law granting all those previously "excluded" from the grandfather exemption a twelve-day period in which to register. Although held unconstitutional in 1939 in *Lane v. Wilson*, the new law had the desired effect of keeping blacks in the state from voting for the next several decades.

During the decades after 1915 the NAACP brought court challenges against other methods of disfranchisement. In 1921 the Supreme Court ruled that primary elections, elections in which candidates were nominated to run in the general election, were not part of the electoral process subject to governmental authority. Six years later the Court rejected the "white primary" in a pair of rulings. In *Nixon v. Herndon* in 1927 and *Nixon v. Condon* in 1932, the Court struck down attempts by the state of Texas to prevent African Americans from voting in primary elections. However, when the Democratic Party in Texas voted to exclude black voters, the Supreme Court, in *Grovey v. Townshend* in 1935, agreed that this was not a violation of the Fourteenth Amendment. The Court found that since the Democratic Party was a private organization, no "state action" was involved. In

1944 the Court again changed its mind on this issue when, in *Smith v. Allright*, it held that political parties and primary elections were part of the political process subject to "state regulation." Therefore, they were also subject to the provisions of the Fourteenth and Fifteenth Amendments. Unrepentant Texas Democrats once more responded by creating an "unofficial" equivalent of the party, the "Jaybirds," and excluded blacks from participation in local party primary contests. Finally, in 1953 the Court saw through this subterfuge and ruled the Jaybird primary unconstitutional under the Fifteenth Amendment.

Another barrier to voting, the poll tax, finally fell after a long struggle. In 1937 the Supreme Court ruled in *Breedlove v. Suttles* that such a tax did not violate either the Fourteenth or the Fifteenth Amendment. The decision, however, resulted in a nationwide campaign to force Congress to prohibit its use. While a number of states acted on their own to abolish the tax, it was not until over two decades later that Congress acted. Passed in 1964, and ratified that same year, the Twenty-Fourth Amendment to the Constitution stated that the right of citizens to vote in federal elections "shall not be denied or abridged by the United States or by any State by reason of the failure to pay any poll tax or any other tax." The state of Virginia, among those states still using a poll tax, attempted to evade this prohibition by confining the tax to local and state elections. Voters had the option of presenting a certificate of residency at least six months before a federal election. But obtaining such a certificate required payment of the state tax ahead of time. The Supreme Court rejected this as well. In 1966, in *Harper v. Virginia State Board of Elections*, the Court held that all state poll taxes were a violation of the equal protection clause of the Fourteenth Amendment.

Despite removal of these barriers, the majority of potential African-American voters in the South in the early 1960s still could not vote. To some extent the campaign to ensure political equality had become overshadowed since the 1940s by the epic struggle of the NAACP and other organizations to dismantle racial segregation. The Supreme Court's 1954 landmark ruling in *Brown v. Board of Education* marked the culmination of the

NAACP's Legal Defense and Education Fund's legal campaign to overturn the Court's 1896 "separate but equal" ruling in *Plessy v. Ferguson*. The school desegregation cases in turn helped galvanize a more widespread civil rights movement. Led by such organizations as the Reverend Martin Luther King Jr.'s Southern Christian Leadership Conference (SCLC), the Congress of Racial Equality, and the Student Non-violent Co-ordinating Committee (SNCC), southern blacks and liberal white supporters sought to end Jim Crow segregation outside the classroom. They used a variety of tactics, from marches and picketing to "sit-ins" of segregated restaurants and other public facilities. In a sense these legal victories voiding specific restrictions merely brought things back to where they had been in 1890–92, just before the Mississippi constitutional convention and the defeat of the Lodge Bill. Voter registration remained in the hands of state government. State and local officials, as they had done in the 1880s and earlier, designed a variety of informal tactics and discretionary devices to prevent citizens from exercising the franchise solely because of their race. In a speech before Congress in March 1965, during which he called for comprehensive voting rights legislation, President Lyndon Johnson described what was happening:

Every device of which human ingenuity is capable has been used to deny this right [to vote]. The Negro citizen may go to register only to be told the day is wrong, or the hour is late, or the official in charge is absent. And if he persists and if he manages to present himself to the registrar, he may be disqualified because he did not spell out his middle name or because he abbreviated a word on the application. And if he manages to fill out an application, he is given a test. The registrar is the sole judge of whether he passes this test. He may be asked to recite the entire constitution, or explain the most complex provisions of state laws. And even a college degree cannot be used to prove that he can read and write.

In fact, Congress had already acted. The emergence of a full-blown civil rights movement in the years after 1948 seemed to focus attention on the struggle to end segregation, particularly leading up to and following the Supreme Court's landmark ruling in the *Brown v. Board of Education* school desegregation cases. Organizations such as the SCLC, as well as the NAACP and other civil rights groups, pursued the parallel goal of ending political disfranchisement through court cases and holding registration drives to get qualified voters on the polling lists. The starting point was the Civil Rights Act of 1957. Compared to subsequent legislation, the 1957 act seems almost inconsequential, but in fact it marked the unmistakable return of the federal government to an active role in the protection of voting rights after an absence of over sixty years. It spelled the beginning of the end for most of the judicial rationales that limited that protection, beginning with *Reese* and *Cruikshank*.

The Civil Rights Act of 1957 created a Commission on Civil Rights, whose six nonpartisan members were to be appointed by the president. Its purpose was to investigate "allegations" of violations of civil rights and attempts to deprive persons of their right to vote, or to have their vote counted, "by reason of their race, color, religion, or national origin." The statute also authorized appointment of an additional assistant attorney general in the Department of Justice to deal specifically with civil rights issues and the act's enforcement. This was crucial, for section 4 of the 1957 act provided the "means of further securing and protecting the right to vote." Congress restored an important historical link by taking the one remaining section of the Revised Statutes dealing with voting rights at federal elections that had not been repealed back in 1893, section 2004, and expanding its provisions. Federal district courts and the Department of Justice were once again given jurisdiction to handle both criminal and civil prosecution of those persons attempting to interfere in any way with the right to vote at any federal election. Justice Department officials were also authorized to seek federal court injunctions, or orders, to prevent or stop persons from engaging in any specified illegal attempts at voting interference.

The Civil Rights Acts of 1960 and 1964 contained provisions which expanded and strengthened the 1957 statute. The 1964 act's most prominent features were its prohibitions on racial (and gender) discrimination in employment, education, and places of public accommodation. However, section 1 of the measure attempted to fill in some of the voting rights enforcement loopholes. It included, for the first time, judicial remedies for challenging the use of literacy tests in restricting or denying voter registration. Unfortunately, for a number of reasons these three measures had only a limited impact on the actual registration of African-American voters in the South. This was especially so in the "hard-core" states like Mississippi, Alabama, South Carolina, Virginia, and Louisiana, where resistance to all federal civil rights enforcement efforts was widespread. Attorney General Nicholas Katzenbach, testifying before Congress in the spring of 1965, reported that in Alabama, for example, black registration had increased only about 5 percent between 1958 and 1964 (to about one-fifth of those eligible).

One of the biggest problems with implementing this new legislation was that, as with the 1870s legislation, enforcement was primarily a reactive process. Justice Department officials could initiate action only when specific violations were brought to their attention or when government investigations had revealed a pattern of discrimination. As a result, federal courts in the South were flooded with cases, many involving small counties or voting districts with few affected voters. The other problem was the active resistance of state governments and officials to the law and federal enforcement efforts. Old habits did not die easily, and southern states had developed an immediate response system to any attempts to keep control of the ballot. For example, when the federal government began challenging the use of the literacy test, defined in the 1964 act as "any test of the ability to read, write, understand, or interpret any matter," states like Mississippi dropped the specific "matter" requirements from their laws (such as the federal or state constitution). In its place they substituted a requirement that applicants demonstrate a "reasonable understanding of the duties and obligations of citizenship under a constitutional form of government." Each time federal courts found these requirements in violation of the act, states would pass new requirements that would then have to be challenged.

{ *Conclusion* }   149

Under the 1964 act federal officials could seek a court order, an injunction, to bring an immediate halt to discriminatory practices. However, proof of such discrimination required materials such as past registration records, polling lists, and the like. Southern states began authorizing, usually in the guise of an economic or space-saving reform, the destruction of such evidence. Another common form of resistance to federal enforcement efforts seemed to be based on a distorted variation of the civil disobedience tactics used by the civil rights movement itself. Rather than perform their duties under possible supervision or observation by federal authorities, southern registrars and other election officials simply resigned, individually and en masse, or took sick leaves or some unspecified leave of absence. Not unexpectedly, such resignations and time off usually came at the most critical or busiest times for voter registration. The transparency of such passive resistance became evident when most of these officials were rehired, or cured, once the elections were over.

By 1965 both government officials and civil rights leaders agreed that, despite a genuine enforcement effort on the part of the federal government, the actual results were negligible at best. Too few eligible African Americans were voting in too few places. Reverend King and the SCLC decided to shift their struggle to end discrimination at the ballot box from the courtroom to the streets. Dallas County, Alabama, and its county seat, Selma, became their initial target. It was an appropriate choice, inasmuch as since 1960 only about 400 black voters out of 29,500 eligible had been registered in Dallas County (compared to 65 percent of the white electorate). During the early part of 1965 a series of demonstrations was held in front of the county courthouse, resulting in the arrest of almost 3,000 protesters. Then on March 7, 1965, the SCLC, along with the SNCC, organized a "Walk for Freedom." As the more than 300 marchers made their way peacefully from Selma to the state capital at Montgomery, they were attacked and trampled by state police on horseback. The marchers were stabbed by electric cattle prods, tear-gassed, and beaten by ropes, whips, and chains. Unlike in Grant Parish, no one was killed, but this time the entire nation witnessed the outrage on that evening's television news. Within a week President Lyndon Johnson appeared in person before Congress in a nationally televised speech. As described earlier, the president called for comprehensive legislation without "delay . . . or hesitation" to eradicate racial discrimination in voting completely. "A century has passed, more than a hundred years since equality was promised," the president proclaimed, "and yet the Negro is not equal."

Within six months Congress had passed the Voting Rights Act of 1965. It prohibited any "qualifications or prerequisite to voting, or standard, practice, or procedure" by a state or subdivision of a state that was used to deny or abridge the right to vote on account of race or color, including poll taxes in state contests. Also specifically targeted were literacy tests and all their permutations, which would come under a complete ban in any state or part of a state where such tests or devices were used and where the percentage of registered voters was less than 50 percent of eligible voters as of November 1964. Moreover, in any state where such a ban was in force, any and all changes in the state's election laws had to be approved by the federal district court in the District of Columbia or by the attorney general. And in those states where patterns of discrimination by registrars existed, or where registrars used resignation or leave of absence to deny persons the opportunity to register, federal "voting examiners" could be appointed to register voters themselves. Violations of the act were subject to criminal penalties and civil remedies in the federal courts and applied to both public officials and private individuals.

Following passage of this new voting rights legislation, there was some concern that even the pro–civil rights Supreme Court and Chief Justice Warren might not entirely support the breadth of federal involvement in the electoral process proposed in the act. South Carolina, with Louisiana, Virginia, Mississippi, Alabama, and Georgia all submitting their own amicus curiae briefs in support, immediately challenged the constitutionality of all of the above provisions of the 1965 act in federal court. But this was not 1875. In *South Carolina v. Katzenbach*, the Supreme Court completely rejected the southern states' claim and upheld the act as appropriate legislation to enforce the provisions of the Fifteenth

Amendment. Writing for a unanimous Court (Justice Hugo Black filed a concurring opinion), the chief justice ruled that the language and purpose of the Fifteenth Amendment and all the "prior decisions construing its several provisions" led to the "fundamental principle" that "Congress may use any rational means to effectuate the constitutional prohibition of racial discrimination in voting." In support of such strong national authority Warren cited Chief Justice John Marshall's famous dictum from his 1819 *McCulloch v. Maryland* decision: "Let the ends be legitimate, let it be within the scope of the constitution, and all means which are appropriate, which are plainly adopted to that end . . . are constitutional."

A portion of Warren's opinion was taken up with the Fifteenth Amendment's history after ratification. While it might be expected that some prominence would be given to the role that the *Reese* and *Cruikshank* decisions of 1875 played in limiting federal enforcement of voting rights, such was not the case. Between a brief description of the Enforcement Acts in 1870–71 and the imposition of state voter tests after 1890, all Chief Justice Warren wrote was: "As the years passed and fervor for racial equality waned, enforcement of the laws became spotty and ineffective, and most of their provisions were repealed in 1894." Although it would have provided a symmetrical and fitting ending to the story of these decisions, no mention of the Reconstruction election cases appeared anywhere in Warren's opinion. In what was, however, a rather unusual ending for a Supreme Court opinion, Warren wrote movingly of the Court's intended consequences for the future of the act. In a kind of counterpoint to author Albion Tourgee's reference to that same future almost a century earlier, the chief justice predicted:

Hopefully, millions of non-white Americans will now be able to participate for the first time on an equal basis in the government under which they live. We may finally look forward to the day when truly "(t)he right of citizens of the United States to vote shall not be denied or abridged by the United States or by any State on account of race, color, or previous condition of servitude."

It would be equally fitting, and satisfying, to show how over the next thirty years, Chief Justice Warren's hopes for the future of the 1965 act and voting rights were completely fulfilled. The act itself was amended in 1970, and its original time limit of five years extended another five years. In 1975 it was given an additional seven years, and in 1982 it was extended once more for twenty-five years (hence that rumor that African Americans will lose their right to vote in 2007). It is certainly true that over the past thirty years thousands upon thousands of African-American voters have been able to register and vote, thanks, in large part, to the effective enforcement of the 1965 act. Unlike the case with the first enforcement efforts in the nineteenth century, Justice Department officials in the 1970s and after tended to complain about too much bureaucratic support, where their predecessors had received far too little. Moreover, the South's political landscape was fundamentally transformed, especially with the election of black officials on all levels. Certainly one of the act's triumphs was the election of the first African-American state governor, L. Douglas Wilder. Wilder's election in Virginia was from a state that, after all, had one of the oldest histories of social and political discrimination and that had participated in the first major challenge to the Voting Rights Act.

The story of the Voting Rights Act of 1965 is by no means over. Like its nineteenth-century predecessors, the 1965 act and its various extensions have not been without controversies and critics. Even after the *Katzenbach* ruling, southern states, as well as a number of northern ones, continued to challenge either specific provisions of the legislation or federal authorities' adverse findings of discriminatory activity on their part. Increasingly, these cases have had less to do with the registration of voters and the question of "who gets to vote?" than with the equally complicated issue of "whose votes count?" Since the beginning of our nation's history state legislatures have been responsible for drawing up the boundary lines for legislative districts, including congressional districts. As early as the eighteenth century some legislatures engaged in what became known as "gerrymandering," the drawing of electoral boundary lines so as to include or exclude particular segments of the voting population. Historically, the gerrymandering issue centered on divisions between political parties and between urban and rural areas within the states. Up until the 1950s the Supreme Court avoided what it called a "political thicket" by giving the states fairly wide latitude in how they apportioned legislative districts.

Ironically, one of the first steps by the Supreme Court into the thicket of legislative apportionment involved race. In 1960 Macon County, Alabama, was one of the most heavily populated black counties in the nation. Its county seat was the town of Tuskegee, home to the famous Tuskegee Institute, founded by Booker T. Washington in the late nineteenth century to educate African Americans. The large population of educated and politically conscious African Americans had managed to overcome Alabama's best attempts to deny them the franchise, and consequently made up a majority of the town's electorate. This was of course intolerable to the state legislature, which redrew the boundaries into a "strangely irregular 28-sided figure." This new configuration placed parts of the majority black voter precincts into predominately white districts and turned Tuskegee into a majority white community. With the assistance of the Justice Department, using the 1957 Civil Rights Act, a group of Tuskegee faculty brought suit against the state of Alabama. In its 1960 ruling in the case, *Gomillion v. Lightfoot*, the Supreme Court completely rejected this subterfuge. Significantly, in doing so the Court explicitly recognized the connection between the Fourteenth and Fifteenth Amendments that had been rejected in *Reese* and *Cruikshank*. The majority of justices found that Alabama's law resulted in a "lack of equal protection through a racially discriminatory electoral structure [and] was a denial of the right to vote guaranteed by the Fifteenth Amendment." The Reconstruction election cases had presumably been laid to rest.

In fact, the *Gomillion* ruling had a number of implications. Two years after the ruling the Supreme Court, in *Baker v. Carr*, became inextricably involved in the apportionment issue when it held that legislative apportionment must be based on the principle of "one man, one vote." In essence, this meant that every legislative voting district had to be equal in numbers to every other district in the state. The Voting Rights Act of 1965 extended federal involvement in this process by allowing racial discrimination in apportionment to be considered as one of the proscribed "tests or device[s]" denying persons their right to vote on account of race. Where once the courts and civil rights advocates worried about literacy tests and poll taxes, now they had to deal with such new phenomena as "invidious racial dilution" and "racial gerrymandering." If states could not draw political boundary lines to *reduce* the impact of increasing numbers of registered black voters by combining them with majority white electorates, could states achieve the same result by creating all or predominantly black voting districts? Some longtime supporters of the Voting Rights Act have seen this latter attempt at "racial gerrymandering" as harmful, and the political equivalent, morally and legally, of affirmative action. Others contend, with equal passion, that the question of legislative and other types of political boundary lines represents yet another attempt in our nation's history to deny and delay true political equality not only to African Americans, but to other racial and ethnic minorities as well.

Despite the remarkable achievements since the 1960s of the so-called Second Reconstruction in regard to African Americans and the franchise, issues involving voting rights and race continue to appear. A recent example of this involves the loss of voting rights for individuals convicted of a serious crime. Historically, many states had provisions for either loss of voting privileges upon conviction of some crime or the absence of such conviction as a prerequisite for registering to vote. These provisions rested on the argument that a person who violates society's rules in a serious way deserves the added punishment of losing voting privileges. Most states also had, and continue to have, a process for the restoration of a person's franchise rights upon completion of their period of incarceration or parole. However, such procedures are often difficult and lengthy. In many states the authority to restore one's vote is given to the governor, who also has the power to grant pardons or commute sentences. Given these responsibilities, restoration of voting rights has not been a high priority for state executives. As a result, in states like Virginia there is a significant backlog of applicants. By one estimate some four million such disfranchised voters exist.

What makes this a Fifteenth Amendment issue is the fact that a significant percentage of convicted felons in some states are young African-American men. Inmates' rights advocates estimate that almost 13 percent of African-American males can't vote because of felony convictions. In at least one state, Delaware, that figure rises to 20 percent. Many of those affected are first-time offenders, or were convicted of a nonviolent offense, most commonly drug possession. Advocates therefore argue that any ban on felons voting is yet another means to deprive African Americans of their vote on account of their race. Given the history of southern states' disfranchising efforts described in this book, including denial based on one's criminal record, this is not an altogether fanciful argument. Congress is being asked to consider legislation that would restore voting rights to convicted felons in federal elections. If such legislation is passed, it is certain that some states will challenge the law in the courts. Given the increasing conservatism of the Supreme Court and its willingness to restore more authority to the states, it is possible that the story of U.S. v. Reese and U.S. v. Cruikshank may well have a new chapter.

1865	Confederate armies surrender Thirteenth Amendment is ratified Southern states pass "black codes"
1866	Civil Rights Act of 1866 is passed by Congress
1867	Reconstruction Acts are passed by Congress
1868	President Johnson is impeached by House, acquitted in Senate trial Fourteenth Amendment is ratified Grant is elected president

1870	Fifteenth Amendment is ratified
	Ku Klux Klan violence spreads throughout
	    South
	Enforcement Act of May 31, 1870, is passed
	State of Kentucky passes $1.50 capitation tax
	    to vote

1871	Enforcement Act of February 28, 1871, is
	    passed
	Enforcement Act of April 20, 1871 (Ku Klux
	    Force Act), is passed

1872	Grant is reelected president
January 1873	William Garner is not allowed to vote in Lexington, Kentucky, election
April 1873	Battle of Grant Parish, Louisiana, takes place *Slaughterhouse Cases* narrows scope of Fourteenth Amendment protections
June 1873	Grant Parish defendants indicted

December 1873	Circuit court in Kentucky overturns indictment of Reese et al.
February 1874	*U.S. v. Reese* is docketed in Supreme Court First Cruikshank trial ends with no verdict
June 1874	Second Cruikshank trial ends in guilty verdict
July 1874	Louisiana Circuit Court overturns convictions
October 1874	*U.S. v. Cruikshank* is docketed in Supreme Court
November 1874	Attorney general moves for hearing of *Reese* after Christmas
January 1875	Oral arguments held in *U.S. v. Reese*
March 1875	Oral arguments held n *U.S. v. Cruikshank*
March 1876	Decisions in *U.S. v. Reese* and *U.S. v. Cruikshank* are announced
March 1877	Republican Hayes is declared winner of disputed presidential contest of 1876 President Hayes removes remaining federal troops from South
1883	Sections of Civil Rights Act of 1875 are declared unconstitutional in *Civil Rights Cases*
1884	Supreme Court upholds federal authority over electoral process in *Ex parte Yarbrough*
1890	Mississippi convention approves poll tax and literacy tests
1892	Lodge Bill is defeated in Congress

1896	Supreme Court upholds racial segregation in *Plessy v. Ferguson*
1898	Supreme Court upholds Mississippi voter restrictions in *Williams v. Mississippi*
1954	Supreme Court rules racially segregated schools unconstitutional in *Brown v. Board of Education*
1964	The Twenty-fourth Amendment is ratified, forbidding states from using a poll tax
1965	Congress passes the Voting Rights Act Supreme Court upholds the Voting Rights Act of 1965 in *South Carolina v. Katzenbach*

Ableman v. Booth, 62 U.S. (21 Howard) 506 (1859)
Baker v. Carr, 369 U.S. 186 (1962)
Barron v. Baltimore, 32 U.S. (7 Peters) 243 (1833)
Bradwell v. Illinois, 83 U.S. (16 Wall.) 130 (1873)
Breedlove v. Suttles, 302 U.S. 27 (1937)
Civil Rights Cases, 109 U.S. 3 (1883)
Cooley v. Board of Wardens, 53 U.S. (12 Howard) 299 (1851)
Dred Scott v. Sanford, 60 U.S. (19 Howard) 393 (1857)
Ex parte Clarke, 100 U.S. 399 (1879)
Ex parte Greer, No. 6200, Supreme Court Appellate Case Files (1872)
Ex parte Siebold, 100 U.S. 371 (1879)
Ex parte Yarbrough, 110 U.S. 651 (1884)
Gomillion v. Lightfoot, 364 U.S. 339 (1960)
Grovey v. Townshend, 295 U.S. 45 (1935)
Guinn v. United States, 238 U.S. 347 (1915)
Harper v. Virginia State Board of Elections, 383 U.S. 663 (1966)
Lane v. Wilson, 307 U.S. 268 (1939)
Legal Tender Cases, 12 Wall. 457 (1871)
McCulloch v. Maryland, 17 U.S. (4 Wheaton) 316 (1819)
Minor v. Happersett, 81 U.S. (21 Wallace) 162 (1875)
Nixon v. Condon, 286 U.S. 73 (1932)
Nixon v. Herndon, 273 U.S. 536 (1927)
Plessy v. Ferguson, 163 U.S. 537 (1896)
Prigg v. Pennsylvania, 41 U.S. (16 Peters) 539 (1842)
Slaughterhouse Cases, 83 U.S. (16 Wallace) 36 (1873)
Smith v. Allright, 321 U.S. 649 (1944)
South Carolina v. Katzenbach, 383 U.S. 359 (1966)
Strauder v. West Virginia, 100 U.S. 303 (1880)
United States v. Avery, 13 Wall. 251 (1872)
United States v. Cruikshank et al., Case No. 14,897, 1 Woods 308 (Circuit Court, D. Louisiana) 1874; 92 U.S. 542 (1876)
United States v. Goldman, Case No. 15,222, 3 Woods 187 (Circuit Court, D. Louisiana) (1878)
United States v. Mumford, 16 Federal Cases 223 (1883)
United States v. Reese et al., 92 U.S. 214 (1876)

United States v. Sapaugh, No. 6482, Supreme Court Appellate
   Case Files (1873)
Williams v. Mississippi, 170 U.S. 213 (1898)

{ *Reconstruction and Black Suffrage* }

BIBLIOGRAPHICAL ESSAY

Note from the Series Editors: The following bibliographical essay contains the major primary and secondary sources the author consulted for this volume. We have asked all authors in the series to omit formal citations in order to make our volumes more readable, inexpensive, and appealing for students and general readers. In adopting this format, Landmark Law Cases and American Society follows the precedent of a number of highly regarded and widely consulted series.

As a work of historical interpretation and synthesis, this study has been based on a variety of sources, and the absence of the scholarly apparatus of footnotes should in no way be seen as an attempt to either ignore the debts owed other scholars or deny readers the opportunity to find out the where and why of the author's information and conclusions. On the contrary, the purpose of this essay is to encourage readers, especially students, to explore further the rich and extensive literature and sources relevant to these cases on their own, to go beyond simply being passive, and perhaps involuntary, consumers and become questioning, critical historians themselves.

The principal primary sources used in this study are the Supreme Court decisions, found in *United States Reports* (see Relevant Cases for specific citations) as well as lower federal court decisions found in the *Federal Cases*. The official documentation for both *Reese* and *Cruikshank*, including the indictments, motions, and lower court rulings is located in the *Supreme Court Case Files, Record Group 267*, in the National Archives (Washington, D.C.). The briefs in *Cruikshank* can be found in Phillip B. Kurland and Gerhard Casper, eds., *Landmark Briefs and Arguments of the Supreme Court of the United States: Constitutional Law* (Arlington: University Publications of America, 1975). Material on the Department of Justice in the South in the late nineteenth century can be found in the *General Records of the Department of Justice, Record Group 60*, National Archives (Washington, D.C.). Useful collections of documents pertaining to these cases are: LaWanda Cox and John H. Cox, eds., *Reconstruction, the Negro, and the South* (New York: Harper and Row, 1973); and Albert P. Blaustein and Robert L. Zangrando, eds., *Civil Rights and the Black*

American: A Documentary History (New York: Simon and Schuster, 1968).

In the past quarter century the subfield of U.S. constitutional and legal history has flourished. Two standard surveys of constitutional history are Herman Belz, *The American Constitution*, and Melvin I. Urofsky, *A March of Liberty*. A shorter introduction can be found in Michael Les Benedict, *The Blessings of Liberty: A Concise History of the Constitution of the United States*. More detailed explorations of constitutional issues and development during the Reconstruction years and after include Harold M. Hyman and William M. Wiecek, *Equal Justice under Law: Constitutional Development 1835–1875* (New York: Harper and Row, 1982); Loren Beth, *The Development of the American Constitution, 1877–1917* (New York: Harper and Row, 1971); and Harold M. Hyman, *A More Perfect Union: The Impact of the Civil War and Reconstruction on the Constitution* (Boston: Houghton Mifflin, 1975). Works that focus on African Americans and the Constitution include Donald G. Nieman, *Promises to Keep: African-Americans and the Constitutional Order, 1776 to the Present* (New York: Oxford University Press, 1991), and Mary F. Berry, *Black Resistance/White Law* (New York: Appleton-Century-Crofts, 1971). Although dated, Bernard A. Weisberger, "The Dark and Bloody Ground of Reconstruction Historiography," *Journal of Southern History* 25 (1959): 427–47, is a useful introduction to historians' struggle over Reconstruction. The most recent comprehensive account of that era is Eric Foner's magisterial *Reconstruction: America's Unfinished Revolution, 1863–1877* (New York: Harper and Row, 1988). Two briefer, but important, surveys are John Hope Franklin, *Reconstruction: After the Civil War* (Chicago: University of Chicago Press, 1961), and Allen W. Trelease, *Reconstruction: The Great Experiment* (New York: Harper and Row, 1971).

On the background of the Fourteenth Amendment as it related to voting rights, see W. W. Van Alstyne, "The Fourteenth Amendment, The 'Right' to Vote, and the Understanding of the 39th Congress," *Supreme Court Review* (1965): 38–86; F. Zukerman, "A Consideration of the History and Present Status of Section 2 of the Fourteenth Amendment," *Fordham Law Review* 30 (1961); and R. Bonfield, "The Right to Vote and Judicial Enforcement of Section Two of the Fourteenth Amendment," *Cornell Law Quarterly* 44

(1960). The historical background of the Fifteenth Amendment has been examined fairly extensively, although not nearly so much as the Fourteenth Amendment. An early survey of voting qualifications and restrictions up to 1918 is Kirk H. Porter, *A History of Suffrage in the United States* (New York: AMS Press, 1971). One of the first monographs to focus on the Fifteenth Amendment is John M. Mathews, *Legislative and Judicial History of the Fifteenth Amendment* (Baltimore: Johns Hopkins University Press, 1909). A comprehensive account that stresses the selfish Republican political motivation behind the Fifteenth Amendment is William Gillette, *The Right to Vote: Politics and Passage of the Fifteenth Amendment* (Baltimore: Johns Hopkins University Press, 1965). But see LaWanda Cox and John Cox, "Negro Suffrage and Republican Politics: The Problem of Motivation in Reconstruction Historiography," *Journal of Southern History* 33 (1967), for a contrary view that highlights Republicans' idealism. The most recent and balanced account of the origins of the Fifteenth Amendment is Xi Wang, *The Trial of Democracy: Black Suffrage and Northern Republicans, 1860–1910* (Athens: University of Georgia Press, 1997). This study is also the starting point for the background of the Enforcement Acts as well. However, W. W. Davis, "The Federal Enforcement Acts," in William A. Dunning, *Studies in Southern History and Politics*, No. 9 (New York, 1914) is the early standard account critical of the acts. Enforcement of the Reconstruction Amendments and accompanying legislation prior to 1876 is well analyzed in Robert J. Kaczorowski, *The Politics of Judicial Interpretation: The Federal Courts, Department of Justice and Civil Rights, 1866–1876* (New York: Oceana Publications, 1985). Two important studies that focus on the early implementation of the Enforcement Acts in specific states are Lou Falkner Williams, *The Great South Carolina Ku Klux Klan Trials, 1871–1872* (Athens: University of Georgia Press, 1996), and Stephen Cresswell, "Enforcing the Enforcement Acts: The Department of Justice in Northern Mississippi, 1870–1890," *Journal of Southern History* 53 (1987): 421–40. Everette L. Swinney, "Enforcing the Fifteenth Amendment, 1870–1877," *Journal of Southern History* 26 (May 1962): 202–18, argues that enforcement virtually ended in 1877. However, see Robert M. Goldman, *"A Free Ballot and a Fair Count": The Department of Justice and the Enforcement of Voting Rights in the South, 1877–1893* (New York: Fordham University Press, forthcoming). Information on the Ku Klux Klan during this era can be found in Allen W. Trelease, *White Terror: The Ku Klux Klan Conspiracy and Southern Reconstruction* (Baton Rouge: Louisiana State University, 1971). Two introductory surveys of the history of crime and punishment in American history are Lawrence M. Friedman, *Crime and Punishment in American History* (New York: HarperCollins Publishers, 1993) and Samuel Walker, *Popular Justice: A History of American Criminal Justice* (New York: Oxford University Press, 1985). A brief introduction to American law enforcement is David R. Johnson, *American Law Enforcement: A History* (St. Louis: Forum Press, 1981). The only full-length history of the Department of Justice is Homer Cummings and Carl McFarland, *Federal Justice: Chapters in the History of Justice and the Federal Executive* (New York: Macmillan Company, 1937). The department's efforts at enforcing federal revenue laws are described in Wilbur R. Miller, *Revenuers and Moonshiners: Enforcing Federal Liquor Law in the Mountain South, 1865–1900* (Chapel Hill: University of North Carolina Press, 1991). Three works that analyze the state of the federal government's administrative and enforcement capabilities generally in the late nineteenth century are Stephen Skowronek, *Building a New American State: The Expansion of National Administrative Capacities, 1877–1920* (Cambridge: Cambridge University Press, 1982); Morton Keller, *Affairs of State: Public Life in Late Nineteenth Century America* (Cambridge, Mass.: Harvard University Press, 1977); and Wallace Farnham, " 'The Weakened Spring of Government': A Study in Nineteenth Century American History," *Journal of American History* 68 (April 1963): 662–80.

The complex political background of Reconstruction in Louisiana is untangled in Ted Tunnell, *Crucible of Reconstruction: War, Radicalism, and Race in Louisiana, 1862–1877* (Baton Rouge: Louisiana State University Press, 1984). The Battle of Colfax, also known as the Colfax Massacre or the Grant Parish Riot, has been examined at length, then and since. In 1875 Congress held extensive hearings on Louisiana as the "Committee to Investigate Affairs in Louisiana," *House of Representative Reports*, No. 261. One of the earliest historical accounts of the episode is Mannie W. Johnson, "The Colfax Riot of April, 1873," *Louisiana Historical Quarterly* 13 (1930): 391–427. Johnson's account has the advantage of interviews with several of the surviving white participants, and the disadvantage of being frankly racist in its presentation. More recent and balanced accounts include Tunnell, above, and George Rable, *But There Was No Peace: The Role of Violence in the Politics of Reconstruction* (Athens: University of Georgia Press, 1984). Rable's account is especially useful in placing Colfax in the context of the violence that permeated Louisiana and other parts of the South before and after 1873. The most detailed account to date can be found in Joel M. Sipress, "The Triumph of Reaction: Political Struggles in a New South Community, 1865–1878" (Ph.D. dissertation, University of North Carolina, 1993). The best account of the Justice Department's response to the outrage and its prosecution of Cruikshank and the others can be found in Kaczorowski, *The Politics of Judicial Interpretation*, cited above.

Kentucky's Reconstruction experience is described in Ross A. Webb, *Kentucky in the Reconstruction Era* (Lexington: University Press of Kentucky, 1979). The role of African Americans in the Bluegrass State is chronicled in Marion B. Lucas, *A History of Blacks in Kentucky*, vol. 1, *From Slavery to Segregation, 1760–1891* (Lexington: Kentucky Historical Society, 1992), and George C. Wright, *A History of Blacks in Kentucky*, vol. 2, *In Pursuit of Equality, 1890–1980* (Lexington: Kentucky Historical Society, 1992). For the background of black enfranchisement see Chapter 19, "Radicalism, Negro Suffrage, and the End of an Era," in E. Merton Coulter, *The Civil War and Readjustment in Kentucky* (Chapel Hill: University of North Carolina Press, 1925). Black disfranchisement is covered in William Gillette, "Anatomy of a Failure: Federal Enforcement of the Right to Vote in the Border States during Reconstruction," in Richard O. Curry, ed., *Radicalism, Racism, and Party Realignment: The Border States during Reconstruction* (Baltimore: Johns Hopkins University Press: 1969). Ross A. Webb's essay on "Kentucky: 'Pariah among the Elect,'" in the same volume is also useful. Two biographies of Kentuckians involved in *Reese* are Tinsley E. Yarbrough, *Judicial Enigma: The First Justice Harlan* (New York: Oxford University Press, 1995), and Ross A. Webb, *Benjamin H. Bristow: Border State Politician* (Lexington: University Press of Kentucky, 1969).

The Supreme Court's evolving procedures and traditions can be traced in Bernard Schwartz, *A History of the Supreme Court* (New York: Oxford University Press, 1995). The most exhaustive, and sometimes exhausting, account of the Supreme Court during this period is Charles Fairman's contribution to the Oliver Wendell Holmes Devise series, *History of the Supreme Court of the United States*, vol. 7, *Reconstruction and Reunion: 1864–88*, part 2 (New York: Macmillan, 1987). The best analysis of the election cases in the context of the judicial doctrines of the Waite Court is Michael Les Benedict, "Preserving Federalism: Reconstruction and the Waite Court," *Supreme Court Review* (1978): 39–79. However, for a contrary view see Kaczorowski, *The Politics of Judicial Interpretation*, above. Chief Justice Waite's career, including his role in the election cases, is examined in C. Peter Magrath, *Morrison R. Waite: The Triumph of Character* (New York: Macmillan, 1963). Two compendiums contain useful biographical sketches of Waite and the other justices: Leon Friedman and Fred Israel, eds., *The Justices of the United States Supreme Court, 1879–1978: Their Lives and Major Opinions*, 4 vols. (New York: R. R. Bowker, 1969), and Melvin I. Urofsky, *The Supreme Court Justices: A Biographical Dictionary* (New York: Garland Publishing, 1994).

The starting point for understanding southern history in the last quarter of the nineteenth century remains C. Vann Woodward's *Origins of the New South* (Baton Rouge: Louisiana State University Press, 1951). Two complementary works that trace Republican attitudes and policies with respect to African Americans and the South are Vincent P. DeSantis, *Republicans Face the Southern Question: The New Departure Years, 1877–1897* (Baltimore: Johns Hopkins University Press, 1959), and Stanley Hirshson, *Farewell to the Bloody Shirt: Northern Republicans and the Southern Negro, 1877–1893* (Bloomington: Indiana University Press, 1962). Justice Department efforts to enforce federal election statutes after 1877 are described in Robert M. Goldman, *"A Free Ballot and a Fair Count": The Department of Justice and the Enforcement of Voting Rights in the South, 1877–1893* (New York: Garland Publishers, 1990). See also Xi Wang, *The Trial of Democracy*, above. Examples of the public debate over black voting rights after 1877 are James G. Blaine et al., "Ought the Negro to Be Disfranchised? Ought He to Have Been Enfranchised?" *North American Review* 268 (March 1879): 225–83, and John T. Morgan, "Shall Negro Majorities Rule," *Forum* 6 (1889): 586–99. The response to Morgan's racist arguments is E. L. Godkin, "The Republican Party and the Negro," *Forum* 7 (1889): 246–57. Also useful is

George M. Frederickson, *The Black Image in the White Mind: The Debate on Afro-American Character and Destiny, 1817–1914* (New York: Oxford University Press, 1971). The battle over the Lodge Bill is detailed in Richard E. Welch Jr., "The Federal Elections Bill of 1890: Postscripts and Prelude," *Journal of American History* 52 (December 1965): 511–26. C. Vann Woodward's *The Strange Career of Jim Crow* (New York: Oxford University Press, 1955) and its many revised editions helped spawn a multitude of studies reexamining the development of racial segregation in the South after Reconstruction. A good example of this is Charles A. Lofgren, *The Plessy Case: A Legal-Historical Interpretation* (New York: Oxford University Press, 1987). The best and most comprehensive account of southern state efforts to disfranchise African-American voters is J. Morgan Kousser, *The Shaping of Southern Politics: Suffrage Restriction and the Establishment of the One-Party South, 1890–1910* (New Haven: Yale University Press, 1974).

There are a good number of studies that trace the judicial and legislative triumphs and setbacks of African-American voting rights after 1910. Richard Claude, *The Supreme Court and the Electoral Process* (Baltimore: Johns Hopkins University Press, 1970) is especially worthwhile in tracing judicial decisions and the background and origins of the various federal election statutes between 1957 and 1970, especially the Voting Rights Act of 1965. A narrower and more personal account of the judicial response to federal election legislation is Charles V. Hamilton, *The Bench and the Ballot: Southern Federal Judges and Black Voters* (New York: Oxford University Press, 1973). The failures and current problems and issues dealing with voting rights stemming from the federal legislation, judicial interpretation, and federal enforcement efforts of the "Second Reconstruction" are analyzed in J. Morgan Kousser, *Colorblind Injustice: Minority Voting Rights and the Undoing of the Second Reconstruction* (Chapel Hill: University of North Carolina Press, 1999). For a contrary view see Abigail Thernstrom, *Whose Votes Count? Affirmative Action and Minority Voting Rights* (Cambridge: Harvard University Press, 1987).

INDEX

Greenback Party, platform of, 128
Grovey v. Townshend (1935), 145
Guinn v. Oklahoma (1915), 145

Habeas corpus, 20, 34, 125
Hadnot, James, 45, 46
Hadnot, John P., 53, 54
Hadnot, Luke, 49
Hadnot, William H., 51
Hampton, Wade, 129
  defense fund by, 37
  on disfranchisement, 2
Harassment, 37–38, 44
  witness, 120
Harlan, John Marshall, 68, 70, 128
  civil rights and, 99–100
  Civil Rights Cases and, 126–27
  federal involvement and, 63
  racial segregation and, 127
Harper's Weekly, Klansmen in, 33
Harper v. Virginia State Board of
  Elections (1966), 146
Harrison, Benjamin, 123, 140
Harrison, William H., 123
Hayes, Rutherford B., 74, 121, 126
  election of, 117
  New Departure and, 118
  rebel rule and, 116
  voting rights and, 118
Hickman, Thomas J., 53
Hoar, Ebenezer, 31
Hoar, George Frisbie, 132, 134
Homestead Act, 29
Hughes, Charles Evans, 3
Hughes, Robert, 112
Hunt, Ward, 74, 97
  dissent by, 95–96, 99, 100
  Enforcement Acts and, 98, 99
  Fifteenth Amendment and, 98
  nomination of, 75
  on punishment, 98–99
  Reconstruction Amendments
    and, 100

Reese and, 75, 90, 126
Huntington, Collis P., 39

Independent movements, 128, 129
Inmates' rights, 156
In re Goldman (1878), 110, 120
Intermarriage, 131
Internet, rumors on, 1–2
Intimidation, 37–38, 122, 133–34
Invidious racial dilution, 155
Invisible Empire. See Ku Klux Klan
Irwin, William B., 53, 54

Jaybirds, 146
Jim Crow segregation, 124, 127,
    144
  end of, 147
  in Kentucky, 142
Johnson, Andrew
  District of Columbia bill and, 12
  enfranchisement and, 10
  freedmen and, 7, 8, 9
  impeachment of, 40
  Reconstruction and, 10, 11, 43
  southern state governments and,
    8–9
  voting rights and, 38
Johnson, Lyndon B., 147, 151
Johnson, Reverdy, 37, 76
Joint Committee on
  Reconstruction, 11, 39
Judicial commissions, proposed, 28
Judicial review, 41, 86
Judiciary Act (1789)
  court system and, 30–31
  Department of Justice and, 25
Juries, excluding blacks from, 140
Jurisdictional issues, 111

Katzenbach, Nicholas, 149
Kellogg, William Pitt, 43, 44, 46
King, Martin Luther, Jr., 147, 150
Kiss-ballots, described, 122

{ Reconstruction and Black Suffrage }

National organizations, African-
American, 144–45
Naturalization, 17
Negro Fellowship League, 144
Nelson, Levi, 51, 52, 53, 81, 84,
105
New Departure, 118, 123, 128–29
New England Suffrage League, 144
New Orleans, race riot in, 43
New Orleans Times, on black
suffrage, 108
New York Times, 109
on *Reese/Cruikshank*, 108
Nineteenth Amendment, 3, 16
Nixon v. Condon (1932), 145
Nixon v. Herndon (1927), 145
North American Review, The, 129,
132, 140
Northern District of Mississippi
and South Carolina, 32
Northrup, Lucius C., 121
on tissue ballots, 123

One man, one vote principle, 154
Ordinary crimes, 55, 84
"Ought the Negro to be
Disfranchised? Ought He To
Have Been Enfranchised?"
(The North American Review),
129

Party bosses, 139
Payne, J. R., 47
Penal statutes, 91, 92
Penn, Clement C., 53
People's Party, 128
Phillips, Phillip, 76
Phillips, Samuel Field, 75
Phillips, Wendell, 10, 77, 80, 100,
129, 130
on Fifteenth Amendment, 78, 79
on voting rights, 9
Phillips, William, 44, 45

Picketing, 147
Pierce, Franklin, 27, 39
Plessy v. Ferguson (1896), 127, 143
racial segregation and, 141
separate but equal and, 147
Police powers, 104
Political equality, 11, 116
demand for, 43
Kentucky and, 61
Political process, 22
state regulation of, 146
Political rights, 38
protecting, 31, 116, 123, 140
Poll taxes, 41, 135–36, 141, 142,
151, 155
equal protection and, 146
fall of, 146
in Kentucky, 64
Pop and Go Club, 113
Popular justice, 24
Populist Party, 128, 129
Prigg v. Pennsylvania (1842), 81,
99
Property qualifications, 135, 142
Prosecuting attorneys, 34
Pullman Railroad Car Company, 133

Race relations, 15, 44, 56, 131
in Kentucky, 142
variety/inconsistency in, 124
Racial discrimination
Fifteenth Amendment and, 113
proscribing, 77
segregation and, 127
voting and, 91, 105, 151, 152, 155
Rainey, Joseph, 13
Randolph, Edmund, 25–26
Readjusters, black vote and, 128
Rebel rule, return of, 116–17
Reconstruction, 10, 144
civil rights legislation and,
124–25
election cases, 5, 152, 154

Silver Republicans, 133, 134
Sit-ins, 147
Sixth Circuit Court, 31
Slaughterhouse Cases (1873), 52, 56, 74, 78, 83, 101, 103, 132
    Fourteenth Amendment and, 87, 125
Slavery, abolition of, 7, 8, 83
Smith v. Allright (1944), 146
SNCC (Student Non-violent Co-ordinating Committee), 147, 150
Social Darwinism, 131
Social rights, 9
    disfranchisement and, 124
Solicitor of the Treasury, 27, 29
Solicitors general, work of, 30
South Carolina v. Katzenbach (1965), 151–52, 153
Southern Christian Leadership Conference (SCLC), 147, 148
    marches and, 150
Southern question, declining interest in, 129
Special interests, 139
Spooner, John C., 134
Spotters, role of, 36
Stalwarts, agenda of, 116
Stanbery, Henry, 37, 41, 68
    on indictments, 69
    Reese and, 76, 77
State action doctrine, 125
State authority, federal authority and, 55
State constitutions, revising, 136
State sovereignty, violation of, 61
States' rights
    constitutionalism, 82
    dual citizenship and, 101
State voter tests, imposition of, 152
Stephens, Alexander, 129, 130
Strange Career of Jim Crow, The (Woodward), 124

Strauder v. West Virginia (1880), 140–41
Strict interpretation, 91–92
Strong, William, 74, 87, 89
    civil rights and, 75
Student Non-violent Co-ordinating Committee (SNCC), 147, 150
Suffrage
    citizenship and, 114
    exercising right of, 69
    impartial, 12
    limiting, 16, 145
    protection of, 18, 43
    universal, 2, 129–30
    women's, 2, 3, 16, 114–15
    See also Voting rights
Sumner, Charles, 38
Supreme Court
    circuit riding by, 72
    constitutionality and, 40–41
    decision-making process of, 88
    Fifteenth Amendment and, 80
    judicial review and, 41
    self-inflicted wound for, 73
Swayne, Noah H., 74, 89

Taft, Alphonso, 110
Taft, William Howard, 111
Taney, Roger B., 108
Teller, Henry M., 119
Teller Committee, report by, 119, 120
Tenth Annual Report (NAACP), 144–45
Tenure of Office Act, 40
Third Congressional District (Virginia), conspiracy charges in, 112
Thirteenth Amendment, 7, 97
    Bradley and, 55
    federal protection and, 124

Waite, Morrison R., 96
   Cruikshank and, 100–101, 110
   docket book of, 88, 89
   on dual citizenship, 101
   Fifteenth Amendment and, 97,
      100, 104
   Fourteenth Amendment and,
      103, 104
   indictments and, 102, 105
   Miller and, 73–74
   nomination of, 72
   on protection, 102
   Reconstruction cases and, 109
   Reese and, 90, 91, 106
   Second Amendment and, 103
   strict interpretation by, 91, 92
   on suffrage, 114, 115
"Walk for Freedom" (SNCC), 150
Ward, William, 45, 47
Warmoth, Henry C., 43, 45, 46
Warren, Earl
   Fifteenth Amendment and, 152
   voting rights and, 151, 153
Washington, Booker T., 154
Washington, George, 25–26
Watson, Tom, 129
Weisberger, Bernard, 4
Wells, G. Wiley, 33, 37
Wells-Barnett, Ida, 144
Wharton, Gabriel C., 66, 68,
      69–70
   black witnesses and, 64
   Cruikshank and, 70
   KKK and, 63

White, Delos, 44, 45
White supremacy, 131, 141–42
Wilder, L. Douglas, 4, 153
Williams, George H., 69–70, 75,
      100
   African-American rights and, 34
   Cruikshank and, 80
   district attorneys and, 36
   on Fifteenth Amendment, 78,
      79
   Grant Parish and, 50
   Kellogg and, 43
   Kentucky and, 64
   nomination of, 39–40
   Supreme Court and, 72
Williams, Henry, 140
Williams, Mrs. George H., 40
Williams v. Mississippi (1897), 140,
      141
Wirt, William, 26–27, 35
Witaker, William R., 53, 76
Witnesses, harassment of, 120
Women's suffrage, 2, 3, 16, 114–15
Woods, William B., 55, 58, 68,
      110–11
   Bradley and, 56–57, 107
   on Congress/voter protection,
      110
   Hall and, 52
   In re Goldman and, 110
   Nash and, 53–54
Woodward, C. Vann, 124, 128

Yarbrough, Jasper, 113